Ant F

MW00790896

Ant Farms Guide

Ant Farms and Raising Colonies of Ants as Pets.

By

Tori Luckhurst

Table of Contents

Chapter 1. Introduction to Ant Keeping from your house.

Ants are wonderful creatures that you can find in any part of the world. Regardless of where you live, you will find ants there. They live in burrows dug by themselves. There are also some that live in woods, forests, tiny acorns, logs, crevices and cracks on the walls. They are available in a huge variety. For many people, these creatures are pests and should not be found around the home. But the truth is that they can be held in captivity for research purposes, fun and as pets. I and a lot of other people are keeping and raising colonies of ants from home and we found them to be captivating and sources of entertainment and wonders thanks to their secret way of living and organizing their habitat. Here, I am going to tell you more about ant keeping, the dangers in keeping and raising ants from home and why you should keep ants. I will also discuss regulations on ant keeping in various jurisdictions.

The Dangers of Keeping and Running an Ant Farm from Your Home

Growing a colony of ants from home is something that any person can do. Be assured that you will enjoy keeping, feeding and observing these little beings building and arranging their colonies just as we human beings do. However, before setting up a formicarium, you should bear in mind that there are some risks associated with ant farming. First, some species of ants sting and their bites are very painful. Thus, if you are keeping such species of ants, you should be very careful in handling them. You need to seal any opening that will create an escape route for these tiny creatures. They can easily escape from captivity and they can find any hole in the ant farm no matter how tiny it is. If they escape, they are likely to enter into your home in search of food.

As a beginner in ant keeping, I wasn't careful with my fire ants' enclosure. I learnt the hard way when my child was bitten by a number of ants that escaped from their formicarium and found themselves inside my daughter's room as they foraged for more food. It was a painful for the little girl which resulted in a hospital visit. An ant's bite can cause different reactions on the body such allergic reaction, itching or a swollen leg or arm (depending where you are stung). Allergic reactions that are rare include, but not limited to, nausea, dizziness, tightness of the chest, swelling of the throat or tongue and troubled breathing.

Besides, some researchers have come up with evidence that certain species of ants such as Pharaoh ants can infect human beings with certain diseases such as staphylococcus, cholera, tuberculosis, small pox, dysentery, pseudomonas and streptococcus. Certain parasites of animals and poultry also live in ants. Thus, if you are keeping ants, you should have a deep knowledge of the species that you want to keep. Don't keep any species that is associated with any infection. In this way, you will forestall any possibility of getting any of these infections from ants. You should ensure that your formicarium is properly closed every time to prevent them from escaping. They can contaminate your food when they find their way inside your kitchen. Some of them also steal seeds from flowers and lawn beds.

As a warning, ant keeping requires a high level of diligence. Though, it will not cost you much money or time to manage an ant farm from home, you still need to be very careful so that you will not expose yourself to any risk out of your carelessness.

Why Keep and Watch Ants

I am sure that quite a good number of people out there do not understand why somebody should keep and watch ants that are regarded as pests in hospitals and food stores. Another significant group of people see ant farms as toys meant to fascinate and amuse children. If you belong to any of these groups of people, I will say that you are mistaken. There are a number of reasons why you

5

should encourage ant keeping and watching. Before explaining the importance of ant keeping, let me first mention that the practice did not start today or even in the recent past. Nobody can actually tell when ant keeping and watching started. But there are historical records to suggest that men have been keeping and watching for many, many years.

The Greek mythology narrates how a son of Zeus – the chief god in Greek mythology – changed into an ant in order to win the admiration of a lady that he was in love with. As recorded in the Old Testament of the Scripture, the Christian Holy Book, King Solomon, the wisest of all the kings of Israel, urged his subjects to watch ants so that they would learn from their ways of life. Some ancient philosophers and historians have also written much about ants and their wisdom. Pliny is a typical example of a historian that wrote about ants' wisdom.

A Greek philosopher called Aeolian likened ant colonies and routes to the buildings and roads found in ancient Greece as well as in Crete. I am sure these writers would not have known how these tiny creatures behave if they did not watch any ant colonies. They have been observed and admired by men for their hard-work, team spirit, loyalty, patriotism, resilience, strength, organization, cleanliness and other qualities.

There are a number of reasons why an ant colony can be kept and raised in captivity. First, they can be kept for study and research purposes. It is much easier to study the behavior and lifestyle of species of ants from home than to do that from their natural environment. When you have an ant farm in your home, your research will be more affordable and less time consuming. You don't have to spend time and money moving from one location to another. It is difficult to see an ant colony in urbanized localities except species that live around the house and in the walls. This is because man, through civilization, has destroyed the natural homes of these creatures.

Besides, many people consider them as pests and kill them with chemicals or other means once they find them around their homes. So, if you are studying ants and you don't have a formicarium in your home, you are likely going to encounter more challenging situations than you will encounter if you have one in your home. With an ant colony growing in your ant farm, you will not be spending a dime on transportation.

There is no better way of learning about the ants themselves than having an ant farm. Maybe you have read a lot about ants, their colony, caste system, colony lifecycle and others things about them. As it is said, "seeing is believing." This means that you will not need any person to teach you what you can see by yourself. You will appreciate all that you have read about ants more if you see it with your own eyes. It is also a veritable means of learning more and becoming acquainted with the various species of ants.

Keeping of ants enhances study about these little creatures. A lot is yet to be known about ants. Though some are deadly and can cause certain health conditions to human beings, there are some good ones that can be of good benefits to human beings. Ants are good natural insect and weed seed destroyers. Some species of ants feed on ticks and other insects. With more research on ants, a lot will be discovered about them and how they can be of great benefits to human beings.

Schools nowadays have ant farms in their laboratory. Due to other school programs, children are not allowed much time in the laboratory to view these little creatures to their satisfaction. Thus, they are happy to have one at home. So, you will make your children happy if you are able to establish an ant colony around your home. Apart from that, having a formicarium will make children fall in love with the science of nature. The pleasure of experiencing nature has been destroyed to a greater extent by civilization and urbanization. Many people today have no opportunity of witnessing life in the wild. They only know of life that grows in skyscrapers.

Consequently, seeing a colony of ants growing from first stage to adult stage in an ant farm will definitely help to ignite the interest of a child in the science of nature as it makes it possible for them to see nature unfold.

However, as I mentioned above, it is important that you go for a friendlier species. I will advise that you stay around any time your child is viewing your ants. You know children are inquisitive by nature. They normally get into trouble or damage things in their attempts to explore the world around them. So, they may also expose your ants to danger, kill them or leave your ant farm open creating an escape way for them.

Ants are also great teachers. Humans can learn a lot from their ways of life. It is impossible or very difficult to observe them from their natural habitat. Nobody can peek inside the ground, under rock, through cracks and crevices on the wall or inside logs and woods. Thus, the best way to see and learn from ants is to have an ant farm. I will discuss this later but suffice it to mention that you and your family can learn a lot from ants' behavior.

Ants are a good replacement for other conventional pets. Keeping certain pets such as dogs and cats sometimes interferes with family activities and causes a lot of distractions to the family. They require a lot of care. You cannot leave them and travel for a couple of days without having a person to take care of them. But this is not the same thing with ants. They don't require much care. You can leave them unattended for days. There is no routine of removing pet's faeces, bathing, taking them to the veterinarian and similar tasks. It is a fun hobby which requires little hard work.

It can be entertaining and fun keeping and watching ants. Both adults and children are captivated by ants' way of life. It is fascinating seeing these tiny creatures perform actions that are human-like or things which some other large animals cannot do.

Raising a colony of ants from home is a good way of teaching children how to be responsible. Given that ant keeping is not very challenging, children will gradually learn how to handle other pets and manage their own ant farm. Children will reap the benefits of this experience later in life as adults when they are faced with real life situations.

Keeping and raising ants from home provides ant enthusiasts the opportunity of knowing and learning about different kinds of ants. Indeed, there are many species of ants on earth. Not much is known about some of them. By keeping ants from home, ant fans will definitely want to try various species and learn a lot from them.

Ant keeping does not require much space. Whether you have a garden or not you can still keep an ant colony as you don't need much space in your home to raise a colony of ants. You may not even require any special space in order to keep ants. You can start with a test tube kept on the table. Later when they are established, you can move them to a suitable container or jar. No special structure like bathing equipment and space is required.

Ants are not expensive to keep no matter the angle you look at it. Unlike dogs, birds, cats and other pets, you don't have to take them to a veterinarian and spend a lot of money. The cleaning of a formicarium is not as difficult as the cleaning of a birdcage, dog cage, or a pen for any other domestic animal. Food for ants is not expensive. You can feed them with leftovers from your table or crumbs. It is also possible to breed living insects for nourishment of your ants.

The above are some of the reasons why you should consider keeping and raising ants from your home.

Regulations on Ant Keeping

The laws on keeping, buying and selling of ants differ from country to country. It may be illegal to purchase, transport and keep ants in certain countries; but such regulations don't exist in some other countries. In the US, the transportation of queens from one state to another is banned. The law aims at ensuring that non-native ant species are not brought into a state. Thus, ant colonies sold in the United States of America do not contain the queens. If you want to raise a colony with a queen, then you have to hunt for her in the wild. Therefore, the essence of the law is to protect the native ants from foreign species as it is possible for alien species to escape from captivity. The law is not directed at a human ant keeper. Consequently, it is not illegal to keep ants in captivity or to hunt for them in nature.

The regulations in Canada and Australia are similar to those of the US. In Australia, it is illegal to purchase, sell or own exotic ants, which are ants that do not naturally live in Australia. The law was made because it is believed that the importation of alien species can have a devastating effect on the local ecosystem. Thus, it is difficult to purchase and ship live insects in these countries.

It is a different case in European countries including the UK. The regulations there protect the native species from human ant keepers. The law forbids any person to sell, buy, keep or own domestic ants. It is also illegal to destroy local ant colonies and nests. However, the rules do not forbid or are silent on owning, keeping, buying and selling of alien species. This is why ant movement, live ant pet trade and stores flourish in these parts of the world.

In light of the above, if you are interested in keeping ants, I will advise you to find out what the regulations are on the importation, exportation, buying, selling and owning of ants in your country before making any move.

Lessons from Ants

Ants are tiny creatures which may be regarded by some people as pests. But having observed them very closely, I will prefer to call them teachers. Yes, they have thought me a lot. Here are the various lessons you can learn from these "tiny professors."

Being focused

To succeed in life, you need to be focused. Being focused means being goal-oriented. Indeed, ants have taught me what it means to be focused. One thing that fascinates me about ants is how they go about their duties. If an ant starts any duty, it will continue with it until it is done. They take time to complete each task. Besides, they are detail-oriented.

How to work as a team

Ants are the greatest team workers I have ever seen. A colony of ants can ward off large animals and predators and kill prey that are far bigger than they are. But their strength is in their togetherness. As a team, they are always able to easily and efficiently accomplish tasks that a single ant cannot do. Ants have taught us that rather than doing it alone, it is always better to join forces with others. Working as a team increases output. With team spirit, we can also carry out tasks that ordinarily we would not be able to.

How to develop a routine

Ants have taught me the importance of developing and keeping to a routine. Many people find it difficult to establish and maintain a routine. Having a routine is like having goals or objectives with defined means of achieving them. You only have to follow these means to arrive at your goals. Though we don't have to be irrational and mechanistic in our approach to life, we can achieve a lot and meet deadlines if we develop and keep to routine in certain things we do in life.

The importance of communication

How often do you communicate with your family members and colleagues? Many people may not have thought about this question before. A closer observation of ants has made me realize the value of communication, especial with regards to decision making and handling of issues. When you have challenges in life or when you need to take important decisions in your life, it is important that you discuss the issue with other people, especially reliable people with deep experiences in life. They will help you to make sound decisions. Besides, you get some psychological relief when you talk to someone about your problems.

The benefits of hard work

Ants are tiny but they are very strong and hard-working. These tiny creatures are able to work for the most part of the day – if not right round the clock. They are strong enough to carry things that are fifty times greater than their weight. This is why they are regarded by some experts as one of the strongest creatures on earth based on their size and weight and what they can accomplish. Their hard-work is the reason they can build wonderful homes under rocks, deep underneath the earth, inside woods and other hard to reach platforms. I have learnt from ants that it pays to be hard-working. If you are hard-working, you will not lack anything and you will be successful with everything you are doing.

Believe in myself

Another lesson I have learnt from ants, which I will also like you to think of, is having a positive image of myself and a strong belief in my ability. Regardless of how large or imposing an aggressor may appear to be or how tough a task may appear to be, ants do not run away from that. They are fearless and approach things with the "I can do it attitude." With such a mind-set, they are always able to surmount any obstacle in their way and complete any task.

Working and saving for hard times

Anytime you see ants in their colony they are foraging for food. They do not consume all the foods they gather. They are able to save some for a rainy day. Normally, ants do not go out in search of food during the winter season. Thus, they save food for such days. Outside the winter period, they work hard and make an effort to gather all the foods they will consume during the cold period within the available time they have. Many people today do not have the saving culture. Thus, they suffer during hard times. Ants have taught me benefits in working and saving for a rainy day. It is not just working and saving, but doing it during a set deadline.

Ants are strong adherents of division of work

If you observe an ant colony very well, you discover that each ant has a specific role to perform for the community. Initially, I was thinking that all the ants forage and scavenge for food. But I was wrong. There are some ants that do not go out in search of food. The workers divide themselves into various groups depending on their abilities. There are those assigned with the task of fighting invaders. They also have groups that build tunnels, chambers and structures for the use of the members of the community.

Some people will be surprised to hear that ants have a strong healthcare sector managed by some groups of workers in their various colonies. These workers serve as nurses and doctors tending to their sick ones and wounded soldiers. They also have undertakers that remove the dead ones or those that are dying from their colony.

As already mentioned above, each ant freely joins any group or carries any function it can. There is no compulsion whatsoever. This I think is a great lesson for humans. In your business, places of work and homes, divide roles and responsibilities according to each person's ability. Don't give any person roles that are beyond their abilities. Besides, individuals in the society should be sincere and willing to work according to their abilities. Your family and business will succeed with all undertakings if responsibilities are shared. Nobody wants to be reminded of their responsibilities.

Healthy lifestyle

There is the tendency for some people to think that ants are not clean because they forage in trash and landfills. But I can tell you that ants have a high sense of hygiene and are even more organized and cleaner than a lot of people. First, their colonies are well organized and arranged. Everything has its proper place. They don't live in an environment littered with rubbish. They have stores in their chambers for storing leftover foods. Species that farm and keep herds have a specific spot in their chambers where they farm. Just like human beings, ants have a dumping ground. All unwanted materials are taken to the dumping site. Interestingly, this refuse ground is sited away from their living chambers and other chambers in the colony. Ants also take time to clean themselves up when they are dirty. I will explain in a chapter the part of their body that does this function.

Ants also live an active lifestyle to maintain the quality of their health. If this sounds like a fairy tale to some people, I would want you to take time to observe them enjoy their favorite sports. Just get good binoculars and then throw birdseed into an ant colony. Observe them very well. Sooner or later, you will see them passing it to each other as if they are playing soccer. They are not taking seeds in as food but rolling it to one another.

You may also see two ants from the same colony charging and coming against each other as if they are fighting. Studies have shown that ants from the same colony don't fight. So, they are not fighting but playing, which may be likened to wrestling. Therefore, if you have not been taking your exercise very seriously, you can learn from ants and start getting some workouts in to improve your health.

Ants are also social in nature. They don't live a solitary life. If you see an ant in a spot, look around, you will like see another ant of the same species there. Sometimes, they also gather, not just to forage or work but to socialize with each other. Take time to look at your ant colony, you will see them using their antennae to touch each other's head as if they are discussing or having a meeting.

Learn to be loyal and patriotic like ants
In my own view, only few animals and insects can be as loyal and patriotic as ants. These tiny creatures can do anything possible to

14

protect their colony. They are willing to die in battle in order to prevent any invader from encroaching into their territory. Apart from that they are always ready and willing to give a helping hand to the members of their colony. Once an ant calls for help or sends a distress call, help will be sent in a matter of seconds. They are not selfish. If an ant discovers a food source, it will immediately alert the rest of the foragers among them.

Before you know what is happening, the foragers will gather around the food. They don't relax there to enjoy themselves. But they will take the food inside their territory for other members to eat also.

Indeed, as an ant keeper, I have learnt a lot of from these tiny creatures. Many people have wondered why ants are able to do things that are similar to human behavior. Because of this observation, it is not uncommon to find people wondering if ants think like humans. They ask such questions as 'are ants capable of conscious thinking behavior?'

The truth is that there is no evidence to suggest that ants are capable of conscious thinking. But through studies, it has been discovered that the nervous systems of these creatures are made up of a lot of neurons which send signals to their brain cells. Experts believe that their behaviors are more of responses to external stimuli. This is why when in captivity, ants are not able to differentiate their formicarium from their natural environment.

Another question commonly asked by some people in many ant forums is whether ants are trainable and intelligent like some other pets. Again, ants are not trainable like dogs, cats and other apes. You cannot give them instructions and they listen and obey you as dogs do. It is also impossible to play with them. This is because of the fact that they cannot carry out any conscious acts.

Chapter 2. Information about Ants

Before proceeding with the discussion on ant keeping, it is pertinent to take a look at this creature to understand its various aspects, as this will be of help to you as an ant keeper.

Anatomy

Having raised different species of ants, I have observed the physical structure of these little creatures and noticed that ants are not the same as they may appear to be. There are some noticeable differences in the body structure of different species even though they resemble each other and share certain common characteristics. The body of every ant has three major segments, namely, the head, thorax, and abdomen. Each part is defined by a tiny constriction. Let's examine each part differently.

The Head

The head comprises of different parts with each having its defined function. The compound eyes, mouth, antennae and mandibles are found on the head which is a very important segment of this little creature's body. With the antenna that moves back and forth, an ant can smell, touch and taste things. This part is bent at its middle in a similar manner the human hand is bent and movable at the elbow. This is why it is sometimes called the elbowed antenna. The antenna is not only a powerful tool for sensing and touching things around, the ants also use it to communicate with each other as it helps them to perceive the smell of the chemical pheromones which they release. This chemical helps an ant to communicate to others that it has found food or that there is danger (this will be dealt with in detail in a chapter below). In a colony of ants, the queen is covered with a mix of chemicals, which helps her workers to identify or dictate her presence.

On a closer look on the head of an ant, you will find that it has compound eyes on the upper surface of the head. Unlike the human

16

eyes, their eyes have different facets. The number of facets depends on their sexes and species. Generally, males have more facets than females. Each of the compound eyes of certain species of ants like Formica pretenses is up to 1200 and 800 for males and female genders respectively. All these facets function together to form a single image in the brain of an ant. The eyes of the species of ants that live in dark places are not very effective than those of the types that hunt and scavenge for food during the day. Some of these types of ants may be completely blind. On the contrary, ants that hunt during the day have bigger and more active compound eyes. You may also come across a species of ant with three simple eyes called ocelot.

Ants do not hunt and grasp prey with their forelegs, instead they make use of their mandibles. They also use them to fight, dig the soil, carry prey, cut and bite. This is why the mandibles are regarded as the most important defence tools for ants. The mouth, which is covered by the mandibles, is another important part used by ants to carry out some fascinating activities. Unlike human beings, the ants clean themselves and their nest mates with their mouth which they also use to eat.

Note that regardless of the observed similarities in structures, the heads of ants are different in sizes and shapes. The lifestyle and role performed by an ant for the colony are determined to a greater extent by the shapes of their head. By merely looking at the face of an ant, expert ant observers can tell you its diet and lifestyle.

The Thorax

The thorax comprises three segments, namely the metathorax, mesothorax and prothorax. There is a pair of legs on each part of the thorax. The major components of each parts of an ant leg are tarsus, tibia, femur, trochanter and coax. Each part of the thorax also contains a pair of spiracles. Each of the genders has a pair of wings on both the mesothorax and metathorax. However, ants lose their wings after the marriage flights. Note that the workers are wingless throughout their lifecycle and they do not have any rudimentary representation of the wings. The thorax, also known as the mesosoma, contains muscles that provide the three pairs of legs of an ant with energy for running. Ants are able to climb, walk upside down and hang on things thanks to the hooked claw found at the end of each of the legs. Besides walking, they also use the legs to feel vibration on the ground. With their two front legs, they are also able to clean their antennae and the rest of the legs.

The Abdomen

The abdomen, which is also known as the gaster, is the last segment of an ant. The abdomen of female ants, including the queen, has six parts while that of males have seven segments. The heart, chemical weaponry for defense and fighting and the digestive system are homed in this segment of the body of an ant. Some ants do not sting but at the tip of their abdomen is a tiny opening through which they spray acid to a perceived threat or prey. There are also species that have a stinger. They inject venom into the body of an aggressor with their sting.

Ants are very similar in a number of ways with other insects. I can tell you, many people may not be able to differentiate an ant from another insect. The petiole is an important part of the body of an ant that differentiates it from other insects. The thorax region is joined to the abdomen by the petiole (some species of ants have post-petiole which comes after the petiole). This part makes it possible for an ant to bend the abdomen in order to spray its poison or sting to an aggressor or a prey (it is only the workers of certain species of ant that have stingers on the tip of their gaster). The elbowed antenna also distinguishes ants from other insects. When you next see an ant, try to spot these two important parts that make them different from other insects.

The entire ants' bodies are covered by the exoskeleton, which prevents water loss and offers protections and support to these little creatures.

Life Cycle of an Ant

Ants pass through four stages in a complete metamorphosis, which starts with the egg and culminates at the adult stage. An ant can complete these four stages in 6 to 10 weeks. Here, I am going to briefly explain each of the four stages.

The Egg

Every ant starts its lifecycle as an egg. The queen lays the eggs which are spherical in shape. The egg's size depends on their species. But in general, they are very tiny. The eggs are very soft. In ant colonies, not all eggs are hatched into larvae. Some are used as food by the members of the colony.

The Larvae

An egg hatches into a larva which is worm-like in shape. Though it has no legs, wings or eyes, it is very active and eats a lot. Adult workers provide nourishment to the larvae in their colony. Given the rate at which they eat on a regular basis, they experience rapid growth, molting and shedding their skins many times in the process. On growing to a certain level and before pupating, the larvae of certain species, such as carpenter ants, form cocoons which are silk cases developed for protection during the pupa stage. Those that do not spin cocoons remain uncovered.

Pupa

The pupa stage could be regarded as a stage of rest during which the growing ants reorganize themselves. All the pupae of species that spin this whitish or tan papery capsule undergo all changes required for proper functioning as a fully-fledged adult ant within the protective covering. In general, pupae have certain similarities with adult ants. But unlike the adult ants, their antennae and legs are pegged to their bodies. Thus, they are not active as adults are. They are whitish at the beginning of this stage but as days go by, they become darker. When all internal and external changes have been completed, they turn into adults.

Adults

Ants become adults when they are fully grown, meaning that no further growth takes place at this stage. The exoskeletons do not allow any further growth. However, you will be able to differentiate a young adult from older ones from their colors. The baby ants are lighter in color than the elderly ones. But they all have the same anatomy and physical structure as described above. In an ant colony, adult ants are classified into three castes with members of each class carrying out a specific function for the good of the entire colony.

Caste System in Ant Colony

The three classes are the queens, males and workers. Let us look at each caste and their function one after the other.

Males

Male ants are born for procreation and expansion purposes. Thus, they are born with new queens anytime a colony wants to create more colonies and that normally takes place once every year. Though they have wings just like the queen, they are not as big as the queens. They have straighter antennae, bigger eyes and smaller heads than other ants in the colony. At a particular time of the year, usually when the weather is humid and hot, they fly with unmated queens in order to mate. This is called the nuptial flight because all the unmated males and queen fly to mate.

Unfortunately, the males do not survive after the encounter with the queens. This is why they are said to have a very short lifespan. Once they are dead, the colony is left with no males. The queens will look for a new nesting place to lay her eggs and establish their colonies. Apart from mating, they perform no task in the colony.

Workers

Apart from the queens, all other female ants belong to the caste of workers. These are larvae that obtained the least nourishment during the larvae stage. It is the members of this class that discharge all duties for the colony except procreation. They are the soldiers, cleaners, farmers, builders and hunters. They do not have any wings. In some species of ants, workers differ in their size which determines the function they perform for the colony. For example, soldiers among the workers have powerful mandibles and big heads which they require for fighting. Workers among these types of species can be divided into two groups, namely, the minor workers and the major workers. The former are smaller in size and carry out daily chores such as gathering of food, cleaning of the nest, feeding and taking care of the eggs, larvae and pupae and the likes. They are also smaller in size.

The latter carry out special duties such as fighting. But there are some species of ants in which workers are of the same size. Generally, workers have a longer lifespan than males, though this varies by species. The carpenter worker ants for example, can live for many years but workers of pharaoh ants have a lifespan of about 9 to 10 weeks.

The queens
The ants that got more nourishment during the larvae stage become queens. They are the mothers of their colonies. Young virgin queens remain in the colony and don't mate with males until during the nuptial flight. When they flight to make, they don't return to the colony. Rather, they move to a new site to establish their colonies. It is during this time that they will remove their wings (but not all young queens tear their wings as we shall see later). This is the only time a queen may cater for a colony. But once, she succeeds in raising her first set of workers, she does nothing again except lay eggs. Queens have the longest lifespan among the ant castes. Just like the workers, their lifespan differs from species to species. The carpenter ant queens have a lifespan of about 20 years while those of Pharaoh ants can only live about two to three years. Generally, they are also larger in size than the members of other castes. The major function of the queen ant is to lay eggs for the perpetuation of the species. Thus, they spend their entire lifespan laying eggs. This is

why they don't come out. The entire colony protects the queen. I will talk more about the queen in another chapter.

Species of Ants

There are many ant species across the globe. In a country, there may be hundreds or thousands of ant species. For example, the UK alone has more than 41 different families of ants. So, it will not be possible for me to list all the known species of ants in the world. Fortunately, there is no type of ant that cannot be raised from your home insofar as you have the right captive home and most favorable environment for survival as well as the right care and conditions are provided. However, if you are planning to keep and raise ants, it is advisable that you keep only a species acceptable in your country or a non-invasive types. Here, we are going to examine only a few kinds of these little creatures.

Camponotus pennsylvanicus

Camponotus pennsylvanicus, which is known as the black carpenter ant, is found in a large number in the US. It is also seen in the UK. This species of ants have friendly disposition. Given its friendliness, a colony of it can be kept in an ant farm and raised from home. The major distinguishing quality of this ant species is their big size. Their heads, abdomen and thorax have a light dusting of gold hairs. In a colony of a black ant species, there are about 350 to 2,000 workers. The workers of black ants differ in their sizes and shape. While some may be about 0.25 inches (0.64cm) long others are up to 0.5 inches (1.27cm).

This family of ants lives on trees. But some may also prefer to set up their colonies in woods and logs used for roofing or for the construction of any other structures in our home. During the summer period, they eat more insects and secretions from insects. They can also scavenge for food around the house. One thing that captivates me about this family of ants is the manner in which they crawl. When they walk, they look like a little black horse. Black carpenter ants are so called because of the dexterity at which they create their homes on trees and logs. Some people regard them as pests because of their energy in creating tunnels through woods.

Tetramorium sp.E

Imbued with tough skin, Tetramorium sp.E, commonly known as the pavement ant, can engage their adversaries in fierce war. They make their homes under pavements and bricks and this is why they are called pavement ants. However, you may also find some that build their colony in grassy ground close to sidewalks. They feed on a lot of things such as leftover food thrown in the garbage, pollen, dead insects and others. Like human beings, pavement ants are good farmers. They rear plant hoppers and use them for food. They are normally reddish-black in color. The exoskeletons are covered with hairs, rivers of grooves and peaks. A full grown adult of Tetramorium sp.E is about 0.19 inch (0.48cm). They are found in Europe from where they were brought to the US.

Tapinoma Sessile

Commonly known as Odorous House Ant, Tapinoma sessile is found mainly in human homes where they move around in search of sweets such as honeydew. They built their nest under and around some features and fixtures in the home such as dishwashers, doormats, sinks and insulation. House ants also live in outdoor potted plants, garbage cans, exposed soil and under rocks. Those that live inside manmade structures are known as city odorous ants while those that live in wooded areas are called country odorous house ants. Surprisingly, they live a different lifestyle. They are not dangerous and dirty. They smell like spoiled coconut suntan lotion for which they are tagged odorous house ants. Their size ranges from 0.09 (0.23cm) to 0.13 inches (0.33cm). Sugar ants, as they are also called, are native to US. Not much has been discovered about them. All I can tell you is that there is a lot of research surrounding them and thus, they are a good species to keep in captivity and observe.

Pheidole spa

Big headed ants are another species of ant that I have found interesting. They don't normally live in an indoor environment. They prefer to make their dwelling place in firewood, mulch, logs, patio blocks and similar protected outdoor locations. They are found throughout the US. So, you are unlikely to see them in your house. But if you see them anywhere in your house, look for their trails under your carpets and along baseboards. I also find their trails along foundations and sidewalks. Pheidole spa are available in different kinds. Some species are dark reddish brown while some are light brown in color. They vary in sizes. The major workers are about 0.14 inches (0.35cm) while the minor workers are about 0.1 inches (0.25cm). Big headed ants feed on seeds, insects, grease, protein, aphid honeydew, dead animals and other kinds of sugary foods. They scavenge on human garbage. The majors of this ant family have big heads and mandibles.

Nylanderial (Paratechina) pubers (forel)

Commonly known as Caribbean crazy ants, these species of ants live in thickly populated colonies. Virtually all the colonies I have observed have thousands of members. Their unique characteristic is their ability to live under different areas and environments such as rocks, soffits of houses, wooden debris, cracks in walls, underground electrical conducts and under any item kept on the ground. Unlike many other species of ant, a colony of Caribbean crazy ants can have more than one queen. They eat various kinds of foods. They may be found in many parts of the world. But in the US, they are mainly found in the states of Texas and Florida. Nylanderial pubers are golden-reddish-brown in color. Their workers are all of the same size.

Lasiusalienus

Found in all the states in the United States of America, Lasiusalienus live in different areas. I have seen them under rocks and cracks in sidewalks. Cornfield ants, as they are normally called, search for their foods in human homes. You may see them at picnics as they move about in search of food. They feed mainly on sweets. This family of ants is among the few classes of ants that have different colors. Some are black in color. You will also find some that are brown in color.

Solenopsis xyloni

The southern fire ants, as they are popularly called, resemble the red imported fire ants. I will advise newbies in ant breeding and farming not to keep this species of ant as they sting. With their venomous stingers, they can kill and eat bees and ground-nesting birds such as bobwhite quail. They can also kill sparrow chucks. If you are keeping and raising them from home, it is important that you secure their farm properly to forestall any possibility of the ants escaping from captivity. Note that they pose great dangers to children. They normally build their colonies and homes under flattened craters in open environments or under damp environments. I have also found some under rocks, small loose dirt mounds in grassy openings, under boards and similar environments. In a colony of this family of ant, there may be up to 15,000 workers. They vary in sizes ranging from 0.1 (0.25cm) to 0.18 inches (0.46cm). They feed on different food items such as greasy foods, sweets, dead insects, seeds and the likes.

Monomorium minimum

Known to scientists as Monomorium minimum, little black ants are very energetic and strong in battle. I find it fascinating watching these tiny creatures bullying and beating larger ants when they struggle over food. They eat honeydew produced by small insects like scales and aphids. They also look for food in household dustbins. If you have them at home, you can also provide them with dead insects and spiders. Little black ants build their homes in outdoor environments in places like under the bark of a tree, under rocks and forests. Some can also decide to build their home around the back yard for easy reach to the food sources. The queens, which are larger than other members of the family, are about 0.12 in.

(0.30cm) in size. The workers and soldiers are normally of the same size, about 0.06 inches (0.15cm). A colony has about 2,000 workers.

Solenopsis molesta

Solenopsis molesta are known as the thief ants. Indeed, they behave as they are called. Despite their small size of about 0.06 inches (0.15cm), they steal food from other ants and humans. Their intelligence in stealing is aided by their small size. Basically, thief ants are golden yellowish in color but you may find them in various shades of this color. They have stingers but given their size, they do not cause any excruciating pain to the person they sting. They have big appetites and feed on dead insects and protein. Unlike other species of ants, this family of ants only steals their food rather than foraging and scavenging for it. This is why they are called thief ants. It can be captivating watching these tiny and crafty creatures sneak into other ants' territories and steal their foods including their babies. They are skilful opportunists.

Technomyrmex albipes

Technomyrmex albipes have a unique anatomy which I admire so much anytime I see this species of ants. It has a dark body but the tarsus in each of its six legs is light in color. Mostly found on the Island of Oahu in Hawaii and south Florida, they make their homes under items kept on the ground. I have also found some that live in dead wood cavities of trees. But they can also live inside a home. In case you find them in your home, check for their nest on wall voids as well as around house plants and flower pots. Unlike a good number of other ants, they do not conceal their foraging trails very well. You can easily find them in an outdoor environment. They feed on sweets. All their workers are of similar sizes. They are about 0.13 inch (0.33cm) in size.

Monomorium Pharaonis (Linnaeus)

This species of ants which is commonly known as Pharaoh ant is another monomorphic species of ant that I have observed. The length of the workers is about 2mm (0.08inch). Their color varies. Some are reddish while some are light brown in color. You will also find some types that are yellowish in color. Though they are found in many parts of the world today, they are native to tropical Asia and North Africa. They live in human homes. You can find them in hotels, hospitals, bakeries, apartments and houses. When they enter any home, they nestle in a place with a stable humidity and heat. I normally look for their home in places like cardboard boxes, heat ducts, under toilets, windowsills and sinks. You can also look for them around pipes and heating facts.

What is the best species of ant to raise from home?

One cannot say with certainty which species of ant is the best to keep and raise from home. This is because there are a lot of ants of different species in each region. Though some ants sting or are invasive, with the right care, dedication, conditions, equipment and housing, any species of ant can be held in captivity. However, before you keep any ant in captivity, it is advisable that you find out what the general characteristics of the species are and also the legal requirements of keeping such ants in your locality. Your findings will tell you whether the ant is the best for you to keep.

Color of Ants

Initially, I was thinking that ants have only two colors. There is no doubt that many people also think in a similar manner. But having observed many ant colonies, I can tell you that there are many kinds of ants in different color variations. Even red and black ants differ in their colors. If you spend time observing various colonies of ants, you will find gold ants, green ants, yellow ants, lemon-yellow ants, shiny blue ants and other colors. I have even seen ants that have a combination of these colors.

Ant Colony at a Glance

I have observed ants for many years. One remarkable and common characteristic of ants is that they live and work together. Ants are very successful and can accomplish feat which most insects cannot complete. They are able to achieve this feat because they are social in nature and have a highly organized society in which each member of the society contributes to the life of the society. No ant can live alone or in solitary. Ants living together collaborate to work for their growth, survival, reproduction and common good. This communal living gives ants an edge over solitary insects. The physical dwelling place of ants, its organization and the social rules governing their activities in their habitat are collectively referred to as a colony.

Before providing more information about ant colonies, I have to emphasize that an ant colony is not the same thing as anthills, which are common sights in the forest and some unoccupied areas. Anthills are mound-like structures made by ants with sand, dirt and other materials dug out by ants as they build and organize their colonies where they nest and hide their queens. Anthills show the exit and entrance to the colonies. These mounds are external signs of the presence of a colony. They are mainly on the surface of the ground. But the main colony goes deep underground. It is even possible to see a colony that has a depth of 25 feet (8.33m).

The Lifecycle and Organization of Ant Colony
It takes only a queen to start an entire ant colony depending on the species of ant in question. It is not as easy as many may think for a queen to establish a colony. It is not all queens that fly out of the birth colony during the nuptial flight that succeeds in establishing their colonies. Thousands of them die along the line. Some fall prey to certain predators like birds, other ants and insects. A good number never mate and thus are not able to establish any colony before dying. Some mated but could not find a suitable nesting place before they die. In other words, only a few queens succeed in establishing new colonies after their nuptial flight. Here are the various stages in the lifecycle of ant.

Founding stage
Just like an individual ant has four stages of development, a colony also has three stages. The life cycle of every ant colony starts at the

founding stage with the queen. The queen mates with a male and afterwards establishes her own colony in a site different from the birth colony. During this stage, the queen fends for herself and her first broods. After this stage, her new workers will take over the management of the colony while she will continue with the laying of eggs to populate the colony.

Ergonomic stage

The next stage in the lifecycle of an ant is the growth stage, also known as the ergonomic stage. This stage is marked by increase in population. The queen lays more eggs to produce more workers for the colony. These workers will take up the responsibility of building more tunnels and chambers in the colony, protecting it, serving the queen, caring and feeding the larvae. This period lasts for a number of years. The first set of workers produced by the queen during the founding stage is weaker and tinier than their younger sisters. Workers with the normal size are produced when a colony has developed, had enough food and increase in population. Apart from size, these workers do not behave in a similar manner with the first set of workers who are known as nanitics. They do not stay away from dangers like their elder sisters who are also very shy. So, the life of a colony is very fragile at this stage as these workers may not be able to handle and ward off large prey. So, if an ant colony manages to scale through this stage, it will certainly survive the rest of the stages.

The queens of some species of ants such as Lasius flatus, the yellow meadow ant, establish colonies in collaboration with other queens. With the collaborative effort of these queens, more first workers are produced. However, after establishing a colony successfully, the queens fight with each other as they struggle for dominance. Only a queen will survive the struggle.

The reproductive stage

The last stage in the life cycle of an ant colony is the reproductive stage. In this phase, the colony has achieved a high level of stability and it is economically strong to produce and feed more babies. It is also during this stage that the queen lays eggs that will hatch into winged ants, some of which are new queens while the rest are males. These winged insects will leave the colony during the nuptial flight to mate and establish new colonies. The time when these winged ants are produced differs from species to species. Some queens of certain species will produce these ants as soon as there are up to ten workers in their colony. But some will not produce fertile ants until their colonies are thickly populated.

The end of a cycle
A colony does not live forever. The lifespan of a colony depends on the lifespan of her queen. Once the queen dies, the colony is about to reach the end of its lifespan because there is no queen to lay more eggs. The workers will gradually die off and the colony will cease to exit. However, the queen has a long lifespan though it differs from species to species. The queens of some family of ants such as Lasius niger can live up to 29 years and thus their colony's lifespan is also up to 29 or more years. But species like carpenter ants and fire ants have a shorter lifespan of about 7 to 5 years respectively.

The nuptial flight in the wild
The nuptial flight is an important aspect of the reproductive stage and it also marks the beginning of the founding stage. Thus, it is of crucial importance that I throw more light on it. The winged insects know when it is time for them to take flight for mating. They have a kind of biological sensor that tells them when the weather is most suitable for the establishment of a new colony. But it all depends on the species. The weather may be suitable for a particular species to fly off and not suitable for another. Some species like Lasius niger prefer to take flight when the weather is warm, windless and humid. Normally, during the nuptial flight, a male will mate with a queen during the early or late hours of the day on bright surfaces such as a white terraced-roof. Each colony schedules its flight at a suitable time.

After mating, the queen will look for a suitable location to build her colony. To dig and create the first chamber of the colony, the queen has to break her wings. When she completes digging the first chamber, she will seal it and remain there for some days in darkness. She will lay her eggs there. However, only a few eggs are laid and hatched at this initial stage since she is alone and has no workers to fend for the young ants and serve her. It takes the eggs between eight to ten weeks to hatch into larvae depending on the species. The queen feeds the larvae with the infertile eggs she lays. These "trophic eggs" are produced by the energy of the torn wings.

However, most species with close genetics do not have their nuptial flight on the same day to preclude or reduce the possibility of mating occurring among the members of their class. The males normally come to the mating ground first before the females. The females are able to find them thanks to the chemical pheromones. A queen can mate with more than one male or just with a male. It all depends on the species of ants.

It is important that I mention here that contrary to the thinking of many people, some new queens of certain species of ants do not take flight. Instead, they get to the top of their anthill and wait to be fertilized by males that come across their location. These new queens do not establish new colonies immediately. Rather, after mating, they go back to their old colony to lay their eggs. There is more than one queen in the colony of such species of ants. There are other species that do not allow their queens to step out of their nests. Mating is done internally.

However, they have their unique way of establishing a new colony. It is the workers that will find a new site to establish a new colony. When they have found a new site, they move there with their queens and build another colony. Also bear in mind that queen ants are not so called for leadership purposes. They are not at the head of affairs in the colony even though they are the most important members of ant colonies.

Nuptial flight in captivity

One of the concerns of beginners in ant keeping is how to control young queens and males flying about during the nuptial flight. Their fear is that their homes will be filled with flying ants. Moreover, there is the danger of getting stung by the ant if your species stings. This should not bother you. Ants normally react and adapt to the environment they find themselves in. Since I started keeping and raising ants, I have not seen queens and males taking flights to mate. They normally wander about outside and in the outworld seeking for mating opportunities.

They come back to the nest when they like. I think the reason for this is that in the wild, they are exposed to environmental and climatic changes such as change in humidity, temperature, photoperiod and others, which make them fly away from their colony for mating. But when they are in captivity, the climatic conditions are relatively the same throughout the year. They do not get any environmental cues to take flight. I notice that a lot of the females become wingless after wandering about. They remain in the colony and begin to act as workers. They will eventually die with the male dying first. However, not all of them will remain inside the colony.

There are still a few that will be able to escape from the colony during the nuptial flight. But if you don't want your formicarium or your home to be littered with wings and dead ants, you have to take the ant farm to a shaded location in your garden or yard where they will not constitute a problem to you when they take flight. Leave the outworld open so that the new queens and males can freely fly out. But this is subject to the laws of your country regarding alien species. If non-native ants are not allowed in your country then you don't have to open the outworld.

The average population of an ant colony

It all depends on the species of ant you have in your formicarium. There are some species of ants like fire ants that can have up to ten thousands ants in a colony. In the case of fire ants, it is even possible for them to establish super-colonies with more than one nest. Each nest will have its queen and workers. Certain species like carpenter ants keep small colonies. Some species of ants don't maintain one nest. They move from time to time establishing nests for temporary nests. Consequently, it is quite difficult for one to mention the average population of ant that can be in a territory. To do this, you have to study your own species.

A colony without a queen

Sometimes people ask if an ant colony can be raised without the queen. Indeed, it is possible to raise an ant colony without a queen. In fact, ants sold by pet stores in the US do not have queens. However, no study has established conclusively how the absence of a queen affects the workers' life. What is certain is that the hormones released by the queen have a mediating effect on the activities of worker ants. But no difference has been observed in the behavior of ants living with the queens and those that are not living with their queens (that is when there is no hormone to respond to).

The major problem of raising a colony without a queen is that the family has no potential of growth. Thus, a colony will not last long considering the fact that workers have shorter lifespans than the queens and those workers are barren. Besides, there is not much you can do to elongate the lifespan of your ant colony without the queen. This is because if you introduce a new queen of the same species in the colony, the workers are likely to kill her. But you can give it a trial following the method advised.

How an ant colony is organized

One thing you will find captivating when you start keeping ants is how organized their colony is. Ants, as already mentioned above, are available in a number of species. Each species has its unique habitat. Some ant species burrow and live underground, while some build their home under rocks, woods, cracks and crevices in the walls of human made structures, in and around certain fixtures in the homes and many other places. Regardless of where they live, they are skilful architects and builders. They are able to make homes with many chambers with the queens occupying the most protected and innermost chambers. I am amazed by their sense of air circulation. You will find certain species of ants that have built-in ventilation systems in their colony. They also have food storage chambers.

Interestingly, there are some species of ants that farm and keep herds for foods just as humans do. They take care of their farms and herds and provide them with nourishment to fatten them. Have you ever seen some species of ants collecting vegetation and leaves? If yes, do you know what they are doing with this vegetation? It is meant for their garden. A typical example of a species of ant that collect vegetation is the leafcutter ant. Don't be surprised if I tell you that they grow nutritious fungus gardens they established inside their colony. Some grow plant-suck insects inside their nest. They eat the sweet leftovers of their herds. However, just like human beings, they put effort together to ensure that their farm does well and give them the required food and nourishment.

An ant colony has a similar structure to a human factory or even society. Ants maintain effective division of labor in their various colonies. Each member of a colony has a specific function to perform for the life of the colony. As mentioned above, ants maintain a three caste system which comprises the queen, males and workers. The workers manage the colony performing various chores and tasks. There are some that fight external aggressors.

However, nobody is given any responsibility that is beyond its capability. For example, the younger ants remain inside and attend to the needs of the queen, her eggs, larvae or pupae. The older ones scavenge for food. The queen leaves the workers to work at their discretion without bossing them around. Each worker carries out any responsibility he or she deems fit.

War with other colonies

Just as human communities compete with and clash with each other over things they have interest in, ants also compete and battle with members of other colonies. There is intense competition for food among the various colonies of ants within the same vicinity. However, the competition can sometimes degenerate into wars. The war can be disastrous leading to the death of many members of the warring colonies. One thing that I would want you to bear in mind is that ants kill themselves more than they are killed by human beings. So, if you are keeping an ant colony, you should ensure that your colony is not invaded by members of other colonies nearby. However, despite being aggressive to a competitor, they are highly friendly, loyal and patriotic to their own colony.

Communication in the Colony

Do you know that ants do communicate with each other? Yes, they communicate but not with their mouths as we humans do. Rather than communicating with mouths and making sounds, ants coordinate activities within their colony, recognize the members of their colony and communicate with each other using chemicals called pheromones. The secretory organs of ants emit up to 20 pheromones. With these chemicals, an ant can tell another where it has found food.

When there is an aggressor or an invader inside the colony, they alert nest mates and call the soldiers for war with the help of these chemicals. The chemicals also help to identify sick and dying members that need to be taken out of the colony. Queen ants also use these chemicals to attract males for mating. They use their antennae to smell the chemicals. Their complex brain system helps them to interpret what ever signal that was sent across through this chemical.

The ants in a colony have a unique odor produced by certain chemicals they emit. With the odor of these chemical, the colony members are able to recognize each other. In this way, they know when an invader or another ant from a different colony enters their colony. The queen also has a unique odor which helps her workers to identify her. Apart from this chemical, nest mates also use vibration and touch to communicate to others in certain situations.

Ant Colony in an Ant Farm

I have observed ants in their natural home and when they are held in captivity. I notice that ants living in formicaria organize their colony and exhibit similar characteristics with ants living in a natural environment. The reason for this is quite obvious. Ants are not humans and they are not able to differentiate a test tube and an ant farm from their natural home. Once they adapt and feel comfortable in their captive home, they will organize it to suit their lifestyle. So, there is no difference in behavior and lifestyle between ants in ant farms and those living in a natural environment.

Ant Behaviors

I am particularly fascinated by ant behavior. These little creatures exhibit human-like behaviors. They have a well-organized society just like humans do. They learn, farm, herd, steal, commit suicide, go to war, and work out, you name it… If you take time to observe these little creatures, you will be captivated by what they can do. I have discussed some of the behaviors of ants above and will also tell you more in the subsequent chapters if the need arises. So, I am going to discuss only a couple of them here.

Ants save for rainy days

Have you heard about honeypot ants before? This family of ants has a particular class of ants in their colony that does not work. They just remain in their nest and eat. The workers forage and provide them with enough and the best food. As they are eating, their body turns this food into sugary liquid which fills up their abdomen. The workers keep fattening them until their abdomen becomes as large as a grape. When there is no more food or during hard times such as winter times, the workers will become hungry. The fattened ants will regurgitate the sugary liquid to feed the hungry workers. However, this method of saving for hard times also causes this species of ants some problems. Some ants from other colonies, especially those that are known for stealing from others often invade their territory to forcefully tap from their sugar sources. These immobile sugar sources are also prey to other predators that will also search for them during hard times. Check the preceding titles to know more about farming and herding by some species of ants.

Community imposed self-sacrifice

Generally, ants are their sisters' keepers insofar as they are from the same colony. But surprisingly, certain ant species can compel few of their soldiers to make sacrifices that can even cause them their life for the benefit of other members of the colony. There is a particular native Brazilian species of ant that compel a few members of their colonies to remain outside the colony and work overnight covering the entrance to their colony.

This species of ants normally starts sealing the entrance to their colony before retiring for the day. But when they get to a point where the opening to the colony is almost sealed and they cannot continue doing that from inside, they will compel a few members of their clan to complete the task from outside the colony. These couple of ants will remain outside the camp to continue the work overnight. A good number of these ants do not survive the harsh conditions they are exposed plus the hard labor. Before it is morning, they are dead. One captivating aspect of this community imposed sacrifice is that these few soldiers accept this task and never leave their duty post until the end. They die so that the rest of the community will have life.

There is another species of ants that can also kill themselves in order to protect other members of their species. A typical of example of such a family of ant is the carpenter ants. They defend themselves by spraying toxic chemicals to their enemies. However, they have to give up their lives in order to do this. Their bodies have two glands with one containing this toxic chemical. When there is an invader, a soldier will sacrifice its life by grabbing the enemy and rupturing the gland containing the poisonous chemicals. Though the chemical will kill the enemy, the ant will lose its life. Apart from using this tactic in battle, they also use it to hunt and kill prey. One will sacrifice its life for the rest to have food.

Vampirism

Have you heard of vampires or watched them in movies? There is also vampirism in the world of ants. Dracula ants are sometimes regarded as vampire ants because of the way they feed. These kinds of ants do not build large colonies when compared with other species of ants. They build their home in rotting wood. They suck the blood (hemolymph) of their larvae. The queen and her workers will bite and tear apart the body of their larvae from where they suck hemolymph in order to obtain nourishment. But one amazing thing about this manner of feeding is that these larvae do not die. They still turn into pupae and fully fledged adult ants. Much study has not been carried out on this species of ants because they were newly discovered in Madagascar by Brian Fischer, an entomologist.

Slavery

Though slavery and the slave trade have been abolished in the human society, it is still practiced by some ants. Are you surprised that ants keep slaves? Yes, there are several ant species like the Amazon ants that take captives and use them as slaves. What interests me about slavery in ants is the manner in which these little creatures go about it. They will train soldiers that will invade other territories and capture their workers to serve them as slaves. But surprisingly, they normally attack colonies with the strongest defence because they already know that their ability to put up strong defence is an indication that they are healthy and strong and thus will make good slaves. Some species do not take workers as slaves. Instead, they invade a colony and take away their eggs and larvae. When they metamorphose into fully fledged adult ants, they will use them as their slaves.

Ants go to school

I know that some people will be surprised to hear that ants go to school just as humans do. Yes, ants have teachers that provide instructions to the inexperienced members of the society. Studies have revealed that ants learn via interactive teaching. It is a process through which a nest-mate teacher tutors a fellow ant so that it will be enlightened. As revealed via studies, both the student and teacher ants are highly sensitive to the each other's progress.

Ants have a sense of time

Ants are very sensitive to time and thus they always make haste to complete a task within a deadline. Given their high sense of time, they normally take the shortest trail to food sources and return to their nest in a similar manner. But the question is how do they know the shortest trails to their home or food source? The pheromones again help them to determine which trail will take them the shortest time to get to their destination. The shorter trails have a strong scent of pheromones.

This is because ants that take these shorter routes go more rounds from their colony to their homes and back to the food sources. Thus, as they are making more rounds, they are leaving more pheromones. This will make these routes have a stronger scent of the pheromones. Therefore, if a bigger food source is discovered, the foragers will follow these shorter trails to these food sources in order to facilitate the transportation of the food to their homes.

Ants are time conscious

It is interesting to know that ants do not like wasting resources or endangering the members of their colony. They are quite aware of how unsafe the outside world is. Thus, they normally send as many foragers as is enough to bring in the available food into their colony. When the food source is very large, they will send out many scavengers to bring the food. But if the food is not big enough, only a couple of foragers will be sent out to bring in the food. But how do they know when there is enough food out there? Ants use a foraging mechanism that is quite similar to TCP (Transmission Control Protocol) in computing and networking. The rate at which foragers bring in food to the colony will tell them whether there is much food or not outside there. Normally, the scavengers search for food individually. If any one of them finds food, it will carry as much as it can to take home. The one with food will drop it at the entryway to the colony and it will be taken into the colony by other workers. If the foragers return more often, it is a clear indication that there is more food outside and thus more foragers will be sent out to help out.

Ants have no leader
Though the queen is at the centre of a colony and every ant there is her workers, there is no leader in a colony. The queen does not issue orders or give instructions and nobody does that. The function of the queen is to lay eggs. Each ant assumes any responsibility that is within its ability to do. Thus, there are no managers to assign tasks.

Ants rest and sleep
Some beginners in ant keeping have noted in some of the forums they belong in that their ants sometimes were inactive and quiet but some other times, they are very active. If you have similar observations, there is nothing to be afraid of. It is not a sign that your ants are sick as some people think. It simply means that your ants are not working at that time. Ants are hardworking creatures. But just like human beings, they don't work all the time. They rest and sleep.

Workers are good mothers
Though workers are barren, they are also good mothers. If you take time to observe ants, you will notice that sometimes they carry their grubs about even though they don't lay eggs like queens. Why are they carrying them about? Ants care for their brood in all stages of their development until they become adults. They feed and bathe them. They also carry them about to help them receive some fresh air. Another reason why they carry them about is to expose them to sunlight. In this way, the grubs will become healthy and develop

40

quickly into pupae and adult ants. Left alone, the queen cannot carry out these functions by herself because of the number of eggs, larvae and pupae that a colony may have at a time.

Chapter 3. Building a Home for Your Ants

Whether you want to start with a queen or a mature colony, you will need a suitable home with the most favorable environment for your ants or queen. If you don't have a good ant farm, your effort will amount to an exercise in futility. You will wake up one day to find your queen or ants dead. So, in this chapter, I am going to discuss the housing requirement of a queen or an ant colony. I will first of all talk about the test tube which most ant keepers used as temporarily home for their ants before transferring them into an ant farm.

Setting Up a Test Tube

The test tube is highly affordable and easy to turn into a suitable home for your queen. Just fill about half or three quarter of the test tube with water and then insert cotton inside it to cover and stop the water from pouring out and to forestall the possibility of your ants getting drowned. The ant(s) will also drink from the water. The cotton also enhances the humidity of the test tube so that the ants will not dry out and die. If you need to increase the humidity level of the test tube, then you have to plug in a small quantity of cotton but you should do the contrary if you want to reduce the humidity level. I will also recommend that you add sand or dirt to make the test tube a natural home for the ant. Put the queen inside the test tube and then cover the opening of the test tube with dry pieces of cotton. It is important that you use dry cotton because it is breathable. Fresh air can enter inside the test tube.

Note that even though the test tube is very suitable for any small colony or queen, you can use other suitable containers as the temporary dwelling place for these little creatures at this early stage of their captivity. What is important is for the ant to feel comfortable and secure there. You should ensure that whatever you are using as your temporary home has an adequate environment. It is important for the container to have a transparent surface or opening through which you can see your ant. Below are some enclosures that can serve as perfect substitutes for test tubes.

Vinyl aquarium tubing: It is very easy to set this up. Just purchase a 10-foot (3.33m) length tube from Lowes or any local store. Cut it into small parts of three to six inches. Use clay, cotton or any other material with similar characteristics to cover one end and then follow the test tube setup procedures explained above.

Prescription pill bottle: This is one of the most affordable alternatives to test tubes as it can easily be obtained from a drug store or a pharmacy free of charge. They have a similar structure to test tubes. The setup method is the same with that of a test tube.

Plaster/ytong/pumice/grout: This is also a good substitute for a test tube. But it can be more challenging to prepare. So, if you don't have good construction and technical skills, I will suggest that you consider using the other options rather than this. On a 6x4 plaster block covered with a piece of glass, you can easily establish and attach 3-6 chambers or tunnels where you will insert tubing through which the ants can get to their outworld and/or their formicarium when it is time to transfer them. This alternative is a suitable option for any person raising more than one queen. It will help you to save money, space and time.

Household containers: Where you are not able to find any of the above mentioned alternatives, you can make use of any household container such as a jar insofar as it is clean. Get a jar and cover the bottom with some dirt and put your queen there. You can even use a cup with the bottom covered with crumpled pieces of damp paper towel. Whatever container you are using, it is of crucial importance that you make the internal environment favorable for the survival of your ants. Remember to make the inside damp and provide drinking water to your ant so that they will not die as a result of dehydration.

Once you have gotten any of these suitable containers ready, you can put your queen or small colony inside it. The queen will start to lay eggs and raise her first set of workers if she is able to survive or adapt to the new environment. This stage is a very crucial stage as the price for any mistake or poor management can be devastating to your queen and make your efforts come to nothing.

Formicaria and Their Types
When your queen or small colony of ants has adapted to life in captivity in their temporary test tube, it is now time to move them into an ant farm. Formicaria are specifically made to suit the lifestyle of ants in the wild. They are available in different types to suit different species of ants. Ant keepers who are good in construction can also build a suitable formicarium for their queens or ant colonies. Whether you are buying one or constructing it by yourself, it is important that you consider your ants' lifestyle and how they would have built their nest in the wild. Then, construct one that will make them feel relaxed and comfortable as if they are in their natural home. Here, I am going to tell you about various kinds of formicaria, how to construct one for yourself if you are a do-it-yourself person and also provide you with tips on how to shop for an ant farm. I will also discuss the temperature and humidity requirements in ant farms

and how you can create a favorable environment for your ants inside a formicarium.

Types of ant farms

A formicarium, which is also known as an ant farm, is an artificial home constructed for keeping and raising ant colonies by ant keepers for a couple of reasons. With these artificial homes, different species of ants can be observed and studied. They can also be viewed for fun from their transparent enclosures. Ant farms nowadays can be constructed with different kinds of materials such as glass, plastic, substrates like POP and others. Given this, there are different kinds of ant farms on the market depending on the materials used in constructing them. They are also available in various designs and shapes. There are some designs that are lidded and those that are open. Designs without any enclosure normally do not have high walls and they are free-standing. But if you have this design, you don't need to have any fear of your ants escaping because suitable barriers are made available to prevent the ants from escaping from captivity.

Below are some types of formicarium.

- **Uncle Milton/Gel farms**

Let me point out immediately that Gel formicaria are not good options for those looking for an ant farm to keep a full-blown or large colony of ants. These types of ant farms are mainly made for children to keep ant colonies for a few months or a year. Experienced ant keepers can also house a colony of ants there for study purposes. You can find them in ant stores such as AntsCanada and AntStore. However, some designs of this type of ant farms are expensive.

- **Plastic or glass formicaria**

As the name already tells you, Glass or plastic materials are used in building this type of formicarium. Usually, thin materials are used in constructing this kind of ant farm. They are available in the form of transparent boxes so that their keepers can see tunnels, chambers and cavities created by the ants inside in order to build a strong colony for themselves. They are filled with sand, soil, vermiculite, sand, loam and sawdust, as well as other minerals

- **Medium-less formicaria**

Many ant keepers use this type of formicarium, which features chambers and tunnels for the ants to wander about and build their nest in. They are normally made from autoclaved aerated concrete (AAC or ytong), gypsum or plaster of Paris. There are also some designs that are made from pumice and grout blended with perlite or any other suitable material that can absorb moisture. Those made from gypsum are stronger and have stronger resistance against mold than those made from POP, even though they have same absorbency capacity. The major distinguishing feature of this type of formicaria is that they do not have dirt, wood, sand or any other material that the ants can manipulate or create chambers in. The One good aspect of medium-less formicaria is that you can provide your ants with suitable materials to build up their nest, refuse site and graveyard with mold formed on them which will not get into the material used in creating the ant farm. This implies that you can easily clean off the dirt anytime you want.

The type of material to be added depends to a certain degree on the type of ants you have. If you want to a keep wood-nesting ant for example, I recommend that you use cork which is sold at a very good price. It is a good water absorbent. Besides, it is very easy to cut. Wood ants can easily make nests in corkboards as it is similar to wood in this aspect. You should not be afraid of your ants eating up the cork. Alternatively, you can also provide your ants with saw dust or wood chips. However, don't use these materials if they are treated with chemicals or pressure as they can kill your ants. I will advise you not to use sawdust or wood if you are unsure whether or not it is treated with chemicals.

Note that ants do not eat cellulose because their body does not digest such materials, including wood. So, you should not be apprehensive of anything. If you are planning to keep and raise a colony from home, I will recommend this type of formicarium for you.

One advantage of this type of ant farm is that ant keepers can customize them to meet their ants' requirements. You can include a couple of layers and chambers to make it more natural or to make the ants feel more comfortable. It is also possible to add a couple of tunnels and chambers to enhance the visual appeal of the formicarium. On the negative side, it denies you the fascination involved in observing ants dig and build their nest. The ants don't build anything here as tunnels and chambers have already been constructed for the colony. If you want to view ants excavating and constructing their houses, you can fill a certain portion of the ant farm with dirt or any suitable material. When you put your ant colony inside it, they will be able to build their own nest, excavate and create channels and chambers. Thus, you will get the excitement as they discharge their duty.

- **Test tube formicarium**

This is one of the simplest formicarium to set up. You will only require a box with a transparent part for viewing the ants and then a test tube. Just put the test tube housing your queen or colony when you obtain them from captivity inside the box and leave her/them inside the box to continue their development. When they increase in population and require more space, you can provide them with more test tubes to build their home there. However, ensure that they are properly prepared as I explained above so that they will find it suitable and favorable for their survival. The good aspect of this makeshift arrangement is that it offers awesome viewing. Besides, you don't need to have any skill in order to construct them. They are also effective and highly affordable.

Constructing Your Ant Farm: Factors to Take into Consideration

If you like being creative, indeed, it can be fun and fulfilling creating your own ant farm. Besides, it is a veritable means of saving money on ant keeping because formicaria are expensive. However, building a suitable ant farm is much more than putting your materials together. To make your ants' home more comfortable, functional and secure, there are a lot of factors that you should put into consideration during the construction. Apart from the construction of the enclosure and the engineering part of it, there are also the science aspects of the project. A good homemade formicarium should have a similar environment with the home of the ants in the wild. Before discussing these factors, I would like to emphasize the fact that each species of ants has a unique way of making its nest. So, an artificial ant home may be suitable for a particular species but not for another. I would also want you to know that I don't know the design of the nest of all species of ants (I only know a few). Here are the important factors to take into consideration if you plan on constructing your own formicarium.

- **Take into consideration how your species make their nest**

Don't just create any design you know. I strongly suggest that you take time to study how the species of ant you want to keep make their nest. I will use the Formica species as an example here. In the wild, Formica species construct a colony that consists of one deep vertical shaft with multiple compartments. Now, if you are building a formicarium for this family of ants, you should think of how to replicate this arrangement in the design of your ant farm. If you succeed, your ants will easily adapt to life in captivity and feel secure because their home in captivity resembles their natural home.

- **Don't overlook the humidity condition of the formicarium**

The next thing to take into consideration is the humidity condition of the ant farm. A crucial question to ask yourself in this regard is how am I going to keep the formicarium damp? This again also depends on the design of the nest or on the family of ant that you are keeping. If the design is for the Formica species, then you have to provide a reservoir on the bottom molded with a lip, given that the nest is 45 degrees or vertically structured. Keeping the reservoir of water at the bottom will replicate what the ants do while in the wild as it makes it possible for the top connecting point for outworld to replicate what happens in their natural home. By placing the reservoir at the bottom, a damp gradient will be created which will turn gravity against the water. Another option is to fit a test tube to a bottom connecting point at one side of the ant farm so that water vapor will pass through it to the nest. The plaster or ytong used in making the enclosure does not get wet in the process. With this setup, chances of mold developing in the formicarium will be greatly reduced. The relative humidity should not be below 40% because Formica species prefer a dry nest.

- **Remember the connecting points**
Another important feature that you should include in your formicarium is the connecting point. A good ant farm should have up to four or five connecting points. These connecting points provide the required elbowroom for hydrating the nest. They also provide the required space to the outworld connections. One of the connecting points should be on the top for the Formica design of ant farm being used as an example here. Each side of the formicarium should have two connecting points to the chambers in case your colony needs to expand.

- **Meet the space requirements of your colony**
When constructing your ant farm, it is important that you bear in mind that your ant colony will soon increase in population. You will not want to start looking for another formicarium to transfer your ants. So, I will advise you to make the formicarium very spacious so that as your colony is increasing, there will be enough space for the new members. You have to first take a decision regarding the size of glass to use. Depending on your future plan, a glass size of 5x7 inches (12.7x17.78cm) or 4x6 inches (10.16x15.24cm) is ok for a

beginner. While following the template, you have to press the chambers and tunnels together. Bear in mind that the template serves as a guide only and you are not obliged to abide by that strictly. You can be innovative and improve the visual appeal of the structure without diminishing the space required by your ants. Increase the 3 dimensional surface areas in order to create enough space for your ants to move about. Build the nestling area to be a little bit deeper to make it possible for the ants to lay brood in heap and then stay on their top.

Let me mention that having enough space in your formicarium to accommodate the future brood of your colony does not mean that you have to make your formicarium to be unnecessarily bigger or have redundant spaces. Ants are tiny creatures and do not require a lot of space to grow. You can even raise a colony of 100 ants in a test tube. Sometimes, I see some ant keepers, especially newbies, purchase or build large formicarium for the simple reason that they will want their ants to have enough space or they want a nice looking formicarium. You don't have to waste your money on what will serve no purpose to you and your ant colony. Besides, if your ant farm is too large, the occupants will turn the empty spaces into a refuse site. It may be difficult for you to reach and properly clean the section of the empty spaces used as a dumping ground. If you are not able to clean any part of your formicarium, surely mold will begin to develop there. So, as a rule of the thumb, you should just build or purchase a right sized formicarium depending on how large your ant colony is.

- **Consider visibility**
Another factor that you should take into consideration when building your ant colony is the visibility or transparency of the material to be used for the construction. The major reason why many people keep and raise ants from home is to be able to view these tiny creatures live their life and manipulate their environment. Thus, if you cannot see the ants through the formicarium, the aim of keeping the ant colony is defeated unless you have another motive. This is why I

50

will not recommend a sand formicarium to anyone. If you have a sand formicarium, you will not see ants move about and perform their tasks on a daily basis. This is because they will surely hide inside the sand.

Regardless of the type or design of an ant farm that you will want to build, if you take the above factors into consideration, you will get a suitable home for your ants. The design I describe using Formica species as an example may be crude because I don't have good technical and engineering skills. But you can look up more designs on the Internet. Definitely, you will get impressive results if you perform a Google search on that. Note that ant farms sold in the pet shop have vents through which air enters into them. If you are constructing one by yourself, you need to also provide these vents so that your ants' formicarium will have enough air.

The Outworld

The outworld, known in ant keeping as a basin, is an important part of a formicarium. It is the outlying or outdoor part of the ant farm through which you can access the nest. The outworld serves a number of purposes, which highlight their importance. It makes life easier for the ants as it provides them with space to explore. It would have been more challenging and difficult for you to clean the nest and feed your colony if your ant farm does not have any outworld. It serves as the foraging area. You can also add color to your ant home by embellishing it. Some people grow flowers there. You can add anything you feel that will improve the artistic appeal of your ant home insofar as it is does not constitute any threat to these tiny creatures.

Outworlds are available in different kinds. Here are the major ones.

Outside outworld
Using the outside world has some benefits. It relieves you of the task of feeding the ants by yourself every day. The ants go out to get their food. This is also cost effective as you will be spending less on

feeding. But I have to point out immediately that there are some risks that are associated with this arrangement. First, it exposes your ants to danger. As mentioned above, some ants take slaves or steal from other colony. If such species of ants are in your locality, they are likely going to attack your ant colony. Besides attack by another colony, you are also exposing them to predators such as ant eating spiders. Though it may be interesting to see your ants fight and defend their colony against invaders, they may be overpowered and defeated. Another problem associated with this method is that it gives room for an epidemic in your ant colony. The ants that leave the nest may come back with parasites or bacterial infections. If this occurs, your entire ant colony will be affected sooner or later.

There is also the risk of the ants escaping. If your formicarium has no outworld and you plan on using the outside world, you have to be very careful and apply strategies that will prevent the ants from escaping to the wild or entering into your home. The best means of preventing the ants from escaping is to prevent the queens from escaping. The workers stay where the queen is. So, if the queen is in the formicarium, the foragers and other workers that leave the nest to accomplish a task for the colony will still come back. So, if you are using the outside world as your outworld, you have to build a barrier which the queen cannot surmount but other workers can pass through. The material to be used for the construction of the barrier should be strong and something that ants cannot destroy. Plastic material will be good for this purpose.

Despite these risks, you may experiment on this. But you have to apply caution. I will suggest that you inspect the environment where the ants are to ensure that they are free from predators and other colonies that can attack them.

Open air outworld
Open air outworld is another type of outworld that you can use. This type of arrangement gives ant keepers some benefits. First, it allows enough air to enter the formicarium. When the environment is airy, it

becomes unfavorable for mold to develop in your ant's living space and the environment. With enough air entering the colony, it is easy for the odor oozing from the inside to dissipate. Besides, having an open air outworld minimizes the task of daily care of ants. It makes the feeding of the ants simpler. With this arrangement, the cleaning of the ant farm will also become easier for you. However, the only problem to contend with is ensuring that your ants remain inside. All you have to do is to provide a barrier to force your ants to remain within their colony. In this regard, you have various options which include the following:

Vaseline: Most ants are not able to walk over vaseline. So, rub some Vaseline right round the outworld. But this option is not a very effective barrier as some species of ant can also pass through it especially when they are panic-stricken.

Baby power and isopropyl alcohol: Mix these two substances together to form a paste. Rub the mixture on the top of the outworld. The alcohol will evaporate quickly and only the powder will stick there but loosely. Thus, they easily fall off anything that touches them, including ants. So, any ants that walk on it will fall back to the colony. However, this homemade paste should be seen as a makeshift arrangement. This is because it does not give a long lasting effect. Some ants can easily get over it. Besides, ants are strong and don't give up on challenges. Thus, they will keep walking through it and falling until it loses its efficiency and potency. I don't recommend the use of this barrier for ant keepers of large colonies.

Extra virgin oil: Many ant keepers make use of this barrier thanks to its efficiency. Apply it on the top of the outworld using cotton balls or a wad of paper towel. Don't immediately create the barrier because the olive oil will be dropping down when it is freshly rubbed on the surface. So, if you bring in the barrier without allowing the olive oil to settle and stop dripping, you are running the risk of drowning your ants. Use a paper towel to wipe the droplets if there are any. Virgin olive oil is very common but some species of ants can also walk through it especially when it degrades.

Liquid Teflon/Insect-a-slip: Given that this type of barrier lasts for some months before degrading, it is regarded as the best. Though it is expensive and also comes in a small bottle, you will still get value for your money because it will last longer (a year or less depending on the usage).

Why is the foraging area not closed?
There is no doubt that some people may be wondering why the foraging area should be left uncovered since the ants can escape into the wild through the open space of the outworld. Besides, leaving the outworld open gives the ant keeper the added task of providing a barrier. But it is always advisable to leave the outworld open. I have two reasons for recommending leaving the foraging area open.

Dumping site: The ants scavenge for food in the foraging area and use a section of it as a dumping ground for waste and carcasses of their prey. They also have their graveyard there. These wastes and dead ants will remain there until you clean them. Cleaning up will be somewhat difficult if the foraging area is closed. Secondly, given the high relative humidity of the entire formicarium, covering the outworld with a lid will create a favorable environment for mold to develop inside your ant home making it stink. So, it is important to make the foraging area airy. To achieve this, you have to leave it uncovered.

Preventing your ants from escaping in the future: Actually, leaving the outworld uncovered is a veritable means of preventing your ants from escaping from captivity. So, there will be a time when the foraging area of your formicarium will be filled up with foragers. If the outworld is covered, they will be all over including on the cover. Some of them will definitely fall to the outside world anytime you lift the lid to provide them with nourishment. Those that fall outside the formicarium will definitely escape and will eventually die because they need a queen to build and populate another colony. But on the contrary, if you leave the foraging area open and apply a barrier, they will not escape because the barrier will prevent them from escaping. You will not have any problem feeding them.

Temperature Requirement of an Ant Farm

Ants do well in a particular temperature. If the mercury goes above or below a certain level, they will be affected, just as it happens to other living creatures. Thus, if you are going into ant keeping, it is of crucial importance that you understand the temperature requirements of the particular species you want to raise. The normal temperature for ants in the temperate region is about 24 degrees Celsius or 76 degrees Fahrenheit. But if the species that you want to raise is from a tropical zone, then it will do well under a temperature of 27 degrees Celsius or 80 degrees Fahrenheit. Also bear in mind that the temperature normally falls at night. Always listen to the weather forecast and if the night-time temperature in your location is going to fall, ensure that the mercury does not fall below 15 degrees Celsius in your ant home at night. Now that you know the required temperature for ant species from different climatic zones, I will advise that you always check the temperature of your ants' living container to ensure that it does not fall below or above. Now, I am going to tell you how to check the temperature of a formicarium.

Different kinds of thermometers can be used to check the internal temperature of an ant farm. A formicarium is similar to an aquarium. Therefore, the small, adhesive strip thermometers used to find out the internal temperature of an aquarium can be used to determine that of a formicarium. But if you don't have such thermometers, you can also use the meat thermometer as well as a probe thermometer designed to check the temperature under the tongue. If your queen or ant colony is still in the test tube, there is no cause for alarm as these kinds of thermometers can also be used to determine the temperature inside a test tube. The question many beginners normally ask me is that if the temperature falls below normal how will they heat up their formicaria? It all depends on whether your ants are still in test tube or are in their farm.

It is quite easy to heat a test tube. Get a motherboard box or just a shoebox (any small box can also be used). Rupture the box so that there will be small spaces for easy penetration of heat. Put the temperature and thermometer inside the box and heat them together. Ensure that there is even distribution of the heat around the test tube. Watch the temperature until it comes to the required level.

Different methods can be used to heat a formicarium. You can make use of heating lamps, heating pads, ceramic heat emitters, cables and others. You may also try any method or improvise. What is important here is the intensity of the light emitted by the heating equipment you are using. Some people believe that ants are not sensitive to red light. This is an old myth which has been proven to be false through studies. Researchers have discovered that ants are sensitive to Scarlet Red. However, each species of ants respond to various shades of red in different ways. Nevertheless, I will suggest that you make use of infrared light bulbs or any darkly colored bulb to avoid stressing your ants over the light.

Humidity of a Formicarium

Each ant species has a unique relative humidity requirement. There are some species that like a damp environment and some that prefer a dry nest. Thus, it is advisable that you find out whether the species of ant you want to keep live in a humid colony or a dry one. However, if you are not sure of what the best air humidity for your ant species is, I will recommend that you provide different moist damp areas in their colony. These little creatures know exactly the best condition for their survival. Thus, they will take their brood to the area that is most suitable for their survival. The humidity condition of the corner that they move to is the most suitable for their species.

Chapter 4. Winter Housing Requirements

Many people, especially beginners in ant keeping, get it completely wrong with their ants during the winter period. It is not uncommon to see people providing heat to their ants during the cold period to keep them warm. They also provide them with food for nourishment. Are these good practices during the winter period? The only thing to do for your ants during cold periods is to help them go into hibernation. In this chapter, I am going tell you what hibernation is, how you can help your ants go into hibernation and why they should be helped to hibernate.

Overview of Hibernation

Hibernation is an important crucial aspect of ant keeping, especially regarding their housing during the winter season. Thus, it is paramount that you learn about it and how to hibernate an ant colony, particularly if your ants are from an area that experiences winter. However, you don't have to bother about hibernation if your ant is from a tropical region or desert unless you want to learn it for knowledge sake.

Hibernation refers to a dormancy state experienced by ants during the winter period. Normally, during the winter period, ants will seal off their nest and remain inside without engaging in any activities such as brooding, foraging, excavation of soil, building of chambers and others. The queen does not lay any eggs during this time. Every member of the colony rests and becomes inactive until the winter is over. In other words, before the advance of the cool period, ant workers bring as much food as possible. When you see ants foraging all the time, it does not mean that they eat all the time. They also store some of their food, which they will eat consume when they hibernate.

When ants are in captivity, they also hibernate during the winter because hibernation is more of a natural process. So, even if you heat their nest during the winter period to provide them with warmth, they will also be less active or even not active at all. Brooding will either stop or reduce. The queen will no longer lay eggs and foragers will rest or work for less amount of time. Consequently, it is important that you allow and help them to hibernate as you keep them in captivity. There will be serious consequences if you don't allow them to hibernate. Workers will start dying and the quality of their health will diminish. However, this effect differs from species to species. Some ants can cope with life if they do not go into hibernation. Despite this, I strongly recommend that you allow your ant to undergo this natural cycle in their place of captivity to avoid any ugly consequences. Besides, allowing them to hibernate reduces the task of caring for them as they will not require anything from you except water. The only problem that the colony may have if they do not hibernate is that the quantity of eggs produced by the queen will diminish after a period of two to three years. This is because hibernation enhances egg production by the queen ants. Now, I am going to tell you how to help your ants go into hibernation.

Hibernation in Captivity

If you have an ant colony, the winter season is the time of the year to allow them to rest and go into hibernation. Since it is a natural cycle, all you need to do is to keep them in a cool environment. You can put them in a refrigerator if you have one that will accommodate your formicarium. Alternatively, you can move them into your garage or any space that is not being heated. You should initiate the hibernation process as soon as the weather starts getting cold. Don't put them into a refrigerator immediately when it is the winter season. In the wild, ants gradually go into hibernation. So, it is important that you slowly initiate the cycle by gradually bringing down the temperature to the extent that it is possible. A veritable and simple means of doing this is by bringing the ant farm to a cool location during late October. They will begin to feel the cool weather and start getting themselves ready for hibernation. The place should be free from direct sunlight during hot days that may occur occasionally during the early beginning of winters. But as winter progresses, you can now put them inside the fridge or a cooler place.

Darken the environment more. As discovered during some studies, ants while in hibernation sleep more in a dark environment than a light one. Don't disturb them any longer. You can only check on them after every seven days or there about to find out if they still have sufficient water. You should also be careful. If it is not sufficiently cold as to make them hibernate, then you should consider lowering the temperature to facilitate the hibernation cycle process. In this case, you have to put them in a cold room or refrigerator to make them go into hibernation. On the other hand, extreme cold can also kill them. So, make sure that they are not freezing. Always monitor the temperature of the room where you keep them with a monitor throughout the winter period. If the mercury falls below 30 degrees Fahrenheit, they are in danger. The temperature during this period should be between 30 and 50 degrees Fahrenheit.

Bear in mind that the nest of subterranean ants can have a depth of up to four feet. The temperature after this point dangles between 55 and 60 degrees Fahrenheit. Though, you are not obliged to bring them to sleep or to a state of inactivity, you can also help them to go into hibernation by lowering the temperature below the normal room temperature. Note that it can be more challenging to bring wood-nesting ants into deep sleep.

What to Do for Your Ants during Hibernation

I have said above that you should not disturb your ants as they sleep during hibernation. It is no time for foraging or working. However, it is possible for a worker to stop resting and decided to scavenge for more food. This is a rare occurrence but it may happen. Thus, if you notice any of the ants moving about when others are resting, you don't have to be apprehensive of anything. There is the tendency to provide sweets for them thinking that they are hungry. You can do that but it is not necessary. If you don't provide any sweets, your ants will still survive. This is because before they hibernate, they store a lot of foods that will be enough for them throughout the period of hibernation as I have already mentioned. Though it may be possible for ants to exhaust their stock of food during this resting period, I have neither observed nor read about that since I started observing ants. Besides, hibernation is a natural process. So, even if they run out of food, nature will take care of them.

So, the only thing you should do for your ants when they are in hibernation state is to provide them with water and maintain the humidity of the nest. If the nest becomes dry as a result of lack of water, your ants will not survive the period. Don't be afraid if some ants appear to be dead during this period. It is a common sight when ants go into hibernation. They are likely sleeping. However, if you think some ants are really dead, don't immediately remove them from the nest. First, bring them out and provide them with warmth. If they are alive, they will wake up from sleep. If they fail to wake, it may be they are really dead. But don't throw them away. Just keep them on a wet paper towel. Leave them there until the hibernation period is over. Personally, I don't bother myself about ants that appear to be dead during this sleeping period. I will wait and observe them until the period is over. Often times, ants that appear to be dead during this period start moving about again during spring. So, even though it is possible for an ant to die during this moment, I will advise that you don't make a hasty conclusion.

Chapter 5. Collecting Ants

In the preceding chapters, I have talked about ants, various ant species, and the housing requirements of ants and other topics of general nature. Now, it is time for me to tell you how to choose the right species to keep from home, how to find and capture them and how to introduce them into their new home in captivity.

Factors to Consider Before Choosing Your Ants

The first thing you have to do before searching for an ant to keep is to identify the species you will want to keep. As already mentioned above, some species are more invasive and deadlier than others. I don't keep any species that I have little knowledge of. I will advise you to know the characteristics of your ant very well. Knowing your ant species will help you to know how to take good care of them. The major concern of many beginners is how to identify their ant species or how to know the species of ants they see around their vicinity. If you are completely ignorant of ant species and their behavior, first get a book on ant species and read through it. The information you obtain there will help you to make a choice.

You can make good use of the Internet. I normally obtain any information I want about ants from online forums of other ant enthusiasts. There are many ant forums on the Internet to join. So, join any one and post questions on things that you don't know and you will get a reasonable answer from members. To identify your ant, carefully post a detailed description of your ant including a number of photos of the ants that show its various sides. A member of the forum will provide you with reasonable information that will help you to identify your ant. In general, here are some factors to take into consideration before choosing a species of ant colony to raise from your home.

- **Your experience level**

Make sure that you choose a kind of ant that you can manage based on your experience level. This is because it is more challenging to take care of certain species of ants either because of their delicate nature or because of how dangerous they are. For example, if you are just starting with little or no experience in ant keeping, I will recommend that you begin with the black garden ant, known to scientists as Lasius niger, as they do not constitute any danger. Besides, with them, you will be able to build up a large colony of ants without much difficulty. This species is also good for children to manage. But if you are an experienced ant keeper and you want a more challenging species to raise, you should consider a red stinging ant known as Myrmica rubra. They are aggressive and sting. They do not develop into a large colony but they can create large chambers and tunnels for themselves.

- **Consider your schedule**

You don't just keep a colony of ants in captivity if you don't have time to care for them. The amount of time required for the caring of ants varies from species to species. Some species may require more attention and time to cater for than others. So, before you settle for a particular species of ant, find out what it means to take care of such a species and then consider your daily activities to see if you will have time for your ants.

- **Consider your resources**

Though it does not cost much to take care of an ant, you still have to put some resources into it. You will need a reasonable space to keep your ants and also money to purchase enough food for them. For space, you can build a home for them in your garage, garden and yard if you have one and it is not occupied. Apart from being able to get the required diet for your ants, you should also have enough funds to purchase the various equipment you will need such as ant farm, refrigerator for storing their food, heating equipment and others.

- **The formicarium required**

You will have to provide a suitable ant farm or nest for your ants. Unfortunately, each species have their own way of building their nest so that they will have a favorable environment to survive in. Bear in mind that some ants survive under a particular type of environment. Consequently, before choosing a species, you should ensure that you can provide the colony with a suitable home. For example, it is not wise to keep an ant colony that requires a hot or humid climate to survive if you cannot provide them a similar environment. They will all die. Again, when constructing a home for your ants, you should also consider yourself. Will you want to observe the ants as they go about their daily activities? Are you keeping the ants to study them or for research purposes? If the answer to these questions is yes, I suggest that you provide them with formicarium constructed with glass or plastic.

Ways of Getting Ants

You can either capture your ants in the wild or purchase them from an ant dealer. Each of these options has its benefits and drawbacks. I am going to discuss them in detail to enable you choose a method that will suit you best.

Catching newly mated queens

I consider this method to be the most economic means of getting and establishing an ant colony from scratch. However, this method will require you to watch out for the day of the nuptial flight which, as has been explained previously, is the day males and queens take flight to mate. After the flight, search for queens that have mated already. Pick a number of them and keep them separately in a test tube. You have to make the test tube environment favorable for the survival of the queen inside it.

Put a little freshwater inside the test tube and then insert a cotton ball inside it to soak up and block the water. Bring in the queen and close the open end of a test tube with some pieces of cotton so that the queen will not escape from there. Cottons have pores through which air will enter the test tube. This is why I suggest that you use it rather than a cork or any other cover that will tight seal the test tube. It is also good that you darken the tube in order not to put the queen into unnecessary stress. I normally use a kitchen towel to wrap the test tube. But occasionally, I unwrap it anytime I want to see how the queen is doing.

The major problem with this method is that there is the danger of catching an unmated queen or confusing a worker with a queen that has torn her wings. You also need to know the physical characteristics of a queen as described above in order to be able to differentiate it from the infertile workers. Besides, it is difficult to tell when a queen has mated because the loss of wings does not necessarily mean that a queen is fertile.

How do I know if my queen has mated?
Mated queens tear of their wings after mating. This is not always the case because some queens still keep their wings after mating. The wings remain until a new colony is founded. In other words, there is no certain way of knowing if a queen is mated. You only have to wait to see if she will start laying eggs. Mated queens will always want to lay eggs to establish their own territory with the coming of the nanitics (the first workers).

Shopping for a queen online
Nowadays, it is possible to purchase a mated queen or an ant colony from a web shop. However, bear in mind that some countries prohibit transportation or importation of ants. Some of these web shops also sell tools for keeping and raising ants from home. I recommend this method for individuals that would want to start raising ants without waiting for the next nuptial flights. It is also a good option for city dwellers where there is no suitable natural environment to search for a queen or an ant colony.

Buying from ant-keepers

Though I have not purchased a queen ant from any ant keeper before, I am aware that some people keep ant queens and sell them to individuals that need it. I heard that some people give these queens away to ant keepers after collecting them during the nuptial flights.

Digging up an establish colony

You can also look for an already established colony, dig them up and transfer them to your ant farm to continue their life there. However, I do not recommend this method for several reasons. First, as you are digging up a colony, you will end up destroying their natural home. But the problem is that you may end up not getting the queen. If you don't find the queen, your effort is a waste as you cannot keep a colony without the queen (if you do, the colony will not live for a long time). Note that it can be very difficult – if not impossible – to find the queen of some species of ants like Lasius. These ants hide their queen in a separate satellite nest, which is far from where other members of the family are. There are other species that build their colonies under rocks and in woods. You can accidentally kill the queen when searching for her on such difficult to get to places. Even if you get the queen alive, you are going to leave some workers without their queen. Besides, some ant species have the protection of the law. You cannot dig up such species or else you will be prosecuted.

Another problem with this method is that it creates some imbalance in nature and also causes some damage to the environment. In the natural environments where ants live, there are other living organisms that also live there. So, when you dig, you will destroy the homes of other creatures that occupy these environments with ants. In some jurisdictions, you may be charged to court for this.

I will also not recommend digging because it can result in the death of a number of members of a colony. A large number of workers in a colony die when they are moved into a strange location as a result of stress. Invading their home and keeping them in captivity in a strange environment can be a huge stress to some of them. Those that cannot withstand the stress will die in the environment. So, be prepared for the deaths of a lot of ants in your colony. On the contrary, it is easy for new queens to adapt to new environments after the nuptial flights as it is destined to start a new colony.

I would also want you to bear in mind that the queen in a mature colony may not live long. This is because it is possible that you capture a queen of a colony that is nearing the end of her lifespan. If this is the case, sooner or later, you will still have to go out in search of another colony. So, to avoid this, you should have a good knowledge of the age of the queen. This is an undoable task with the naked eye. It is a matter for investigation in a proper lab.

Here are some precautions to take and ideas to bear in mind when you go out in search of a queen or ant colony.

- If you prefer this method, then you have to use proper tools and only dig in a location where digging is not prohibited.

- Some ants are aggressive and sting in order to protect their territory. I will suggest that you avoid such types of ants. Look for species that do not sting.

- Hunt for ants at the right time of the year. Most ant species normally have their nuptial flight during the first rain of the summer season. This is the best time to hunt for ants. You can also hunt for ants during the spring as they are also active during this time of the year. I will advise you not to go out in search of ants during the winter season. This is because most species of ants are almost inactive. They self-hibernate themselves.

- Don't capture the queen alone. I don't advise people to keep a queen from a mature colony alone. If the queen is captured alone, it is unlikely for the her to survive captivity in solitary. Since after raising her first brood in her new colonies, the queen is being served and pampered by all members of her colony. If you take her alone, it means that she will be doing all the tasks by herself. The stress of serving herself can be too much for her and she may die out of frustration.

- When digging, do it right and ensure that no damage is done to the habitat of other creatures living under the environment with the ant colony you want to capture.

- Despite the various problems with digging, I will recommend it for any person that wants to keep a colony of polygynous species. If you dig a portion, the remaining portion will continue to grow, multiply and perpetuate the species. Thus, you will still be able to catch a queen and some of her workers from the species in the future.

Now you know the various ways of getting your ants, nothing will stop you from building your ant colony. Be careful when hunting for ants in the wild. As already mentioned above, some ants have stingers for delivering painful stings and venom inside any perceived threat while some ants spread deadly acid to their aggressors. So, don't keep dangerous ants unless you have experience with these little creatures. Besides, no matter the family of ants you want, make sure that you hunt for them with the right materials and equipment. Don't use bare hands to hold any ants unless you are very sure that it is harmless. Wear gloves and use trowels or spoons to collect the ants. Also warn your children not to touch ants with their naked hands.

Materials and equipment needed for ant hunting

If you are going for ant hunting, you will require the following materials and equipment:

- a trowel and a spade for digging the soil

- a spoon for collecting the ants (or the queen)

- a container to put the soil

- a container or test tube to keep the ant

- gloves

- a suitable pair of boots, hat and other outer wear

Tips for Finding an Ant colony

For many people, finding an ant colony is as easy as ABC as you will only have to discover their trail and follow it to get to their colony. But in reality, it is difficult to find the home of these little creatures. Some of them have a special location where they hide their queens. Besides, they also build their nest deep inside the ground, rocks, logs or manmade structures. Here are some of the tricks I employ in finding an ant colony.

Trail them: Whenever you see an ant moving up and down, it is either searching for food or returning home. A worker ant that finds food normally leads other members of the colony to the food source through a trail of pheromones it deposited on its path from the nest to the food source. So, if you are searching for an ant colony, I suggest that you look for this trail and follow it. But to do so, you need patience, determination and time as the trail can be long. If the trail passes through an area that you will not be able to get to, there is no cause for alarm. Ants normally change their paths overtime and get to a food source taking the nearest route. I have developed a method of finding the shortest trails to their colony. Just put sweet bait like jam, jelly or honey diluted with water inside a plastic bag. The ants will create a shorter route from their nest to the new food. In this way, it will be easier for you to find their nest.

Look for them at night: Though ants scavenge at any time of the day, they spend more time doing so at night. So, you have more chances of trailing them to their nest at night. But you will require a light touch. Check your dust bins and food containers to check for ants. I will recommend that you keep some sweeteners in your refuse container. If there is ant colony nearby, the workers will find the food and pull it into their colony. As they gather around the food to bring it inside their colony, you can trace them to their dwelling place.

Check for piles of sawdust: Piles of sawdust are physical indicator of the presence of a colony of carpenter ants. So, if you are interested in keeping this species of ant, then you have to look for piles of sawdust around your homes in corners that are most humid such as basement, attic, wooden windowsills and door frames, gutters, outside steps, bathrooms, leaky pipes and laundry rooms. If there are rotting trees nearby, also check for this indicator. If you find any, look closely around to see if you can see small holes, cracks and crevices. If you find any, it is most likely going to be the entrance to the colony of a carpenter ant.

Listen to hear their movement: Some ants, such as carpenter ants, make some sound as they move about. So, at the quiet moment of the night, listen very carefully for a slight clicking sound. Ants react to vibrations. So, you can strike your walls and place a stethoscope there to enable you to hear the sound if they are there. If you hear any sound, check the side where the sound is coming from to see if you can find any ants there.

Check for them at rarely visited living spaces: Take time to check for ant colonies in and around your home. Pay more attention to rooms, closets, bedroom, crevices, cracks, foundation walls and other areas that you seldom visit. Ants don't like getting exposed. They like living in a quiet location.

A look at the Queen

I consider the queen as the most important member of any ant colony because all activities of their habitation are centered on her. She is the mother of all and all members of the colony are at her service. The soldiers can fight to the death in order to protect her. Once a colony feels threatened, all members will fight to defend her. The workers look for food for her nourishment. Besides, you can build a large colony of ants just with one mated queen but you cannot raise any ant colony with workers or any members of other castes in the ant's kingdom. Thus, it is important that I spend more time on this important member of an ant colony. Let us begin our discussion with the types of queens.

Types of queens

Just as we have different species of ants, there are also various kinds of queens. Here I am going to explain the three different types of queens.

Fully claustral queens

Queens in this class do not require much care and thus they are the easiest to keep. All you need is to provide them a suitable living environment which should be humid. You should also keep them in a quiet place free from any disturbance. Keep a fully claustral queen in her new environment and leave her for a month without any food. She obtains nourishment internally from the fat and food stores in the body. Additionally, the wing muscles are also metabolized to provide nourishment to the body. Fully claustral queens have their unique physical structure. Though their heads are smaller, they are generally larger than semi-claustral queens. They spend their life in the nest. They neither scavenge for food nor fight. This explains why nature gave them small heads.

Semi-claustral queens

Queens in this category start searching for their food after their nuptial flight until they are able to establish a colony of their own. They are not as fat as the other queens. It can be more challenging to keep this kind of queen as they have special kinds of food, which should consist mainly of sugars and insects. If you are just starting, I will recommend that you start with a fully claustral queen rather than beginning with a queen in this category. Despite all the challenges associated with the raising of these classes of queen, the fun and fascination you will get as you observe the queen establishing and organizing her new empire will be your reward.

Social parasites

These groups of queens are as big and strongly built as the fully-claustral queen but their heads and mandibles are bigger when compared with those of other kinds of queens. They are called social parasites because of the manner in which they establish their own colony. A queen of this type cannot build a colony from scratch. Instead, she will enter another colony of ants she prefers, attacks and kills the queen there. The workers, having lost their queen, will now serve her. She will establish her colony there. In other words, they require workers in order to establish a new colony.

Raising a social parasite queen can be somewhat tricky, as you will have to first identify and get her preferred workers. If you are not experienced with ants, I will advise you not to keep this type of queen. This is because if you make a wrong choice of workers for her, you expose her to danger. She can be killed by the host workers. You can only succeed in raising an ant colony with a social parasite queen if you are able to get the right host and that will require expertise. The manner in which you introduce the queen to the host is also very crucial. Here are the tips I normally apply whenever I want to keep and raise a colony of ants with a social parasite queen.

First, I get the workers from their colony and keep them for a while in a refrigerator. You should also keep the queen in the refrigerator to weaken and make her less aggressive. After a while, introduce one worker to the same test tube or container where the queen is. Some social parasite queens will first of all kill a worker so that she will be able to access the colony using the scent of her victim. So, if you discover that the first worker you introduce is dead, you should not have any worry, as this is normal.

Now, I will introduce another worker and observe the reaction of the queen towards this worker. If they fight each other, then I have to bring out the worker and reintroduce her another time. If no fight ensues between them, it is an indication that they are getting on well with each other. Leave them together for a couple of days so that they will get used to each other very well and the scent of the worker will permeate the queen. Now, it is time to introduce other workers.

Please bear in mind that some types of social parasite queens cannot carry out any nest activities by themselves or alone. They require workers to assist them. To be successful with a queen in this family, you have to ensure that the enslaved workforce is sufficient. This will require you to keep providing the queen with hosts on regular basis. You may consider raising a colony of the host of your queen and from there, you will get workforce for your queen. I have not tried this myself but I think it will work.

Introducing Your Ants into Their Home

As I have already mentioned above, if you don't have a suitable ant farm for your ants, they will definitely die. It does not have to be expensive, but it has to be constructed to suit the lifestyle of the species of ants you want to raise inside it. Now that you have collected your queen or ant colony, it is time to move them from the storage container or test tube to their home. It is quite easy to transfer ants to an ant farm or a new home.

The first thing you should do is to inspect your formicarium to ensure that there is no escape hole for the ants. Of course, I believe you should know that ants are very skilful in escaping from enclosures through any opening they can find. First, they are tiny and any tiny hole can provide a good exit for them. Secondly, they walk through edges and smooth surfaces without falling off. So, you need to go the extra mile to prevent them from escaping.

You can find out if your formicarium has a hole with these simple steps. Clean up the outside very well making sure there is no moist anywhere. Then pour some quantity of water inside the formicarium. Turn the ant farm to various sides so that the water will go right round it. Inspect the outside to see if there are any leaks. If there is no leak, you are ready to continue with other arrangements. Now, you have to prepare your formicarium to make the environment suitable for the ants. A good ant farm should have a nesting area and a foraging area. There should also be a container of water for the ants to drink. So, ensure that your formicarium has all these important components before you introduce your ants. Note, formicarium does not have one design. What is important is for it to have the basic components and suit the lifestyle of the ants inside it. When everything is ok, you can introduce your ants.

There are a number of ways of introducing your queen and her founding brood into a larger ant farm. I will discuss a few of these methods here. The structure of your formicarium will also determine how the ant will be introduced into it. If you purchase a ready-made product from a store, read the manufacturer's guide to find out how best to move the ants into it.

Putting the test tube containing the ants in a refrigerator before transferring them in a formicarium is a nice option if your ants are aggressive or stinging types. Put the storage container or test tube inside a refrigerator. Remaining in a very cool environment of a fridge will weaken and slow down the ants. Once they are weak, you can bring them out of the container and quickly transfer the queen and her brood inside your formicarium. Don't leave the ants for a very long time inside the fridge. Leaving them there for a minute or two will be ok. Your ants may die if they stay longer than two minutes in a refrigerator. Make sure that you wear gloves when you are transferring the ants into their homes.

You can also allow the ants to move into the ant farm by themselves. This can easily be achieved. First, make the nest area dark by covering it. Then keep the container or test tube containing the ants closer to the formicarium with the uncovered side positioned close or connected to access the opening or tube of the ant farm. Flash a bright light to the test tube to make them uncomfortable. Once they are uncomfortable, they will start moving out to look for a more comfortable location. As they move, they will be attracted by the darkened nest. You can also use a reptile heating cable to apply heat to the test tube. But you have to be very careful here to avoid overheating the test tube, which will cause the death of the ants. Just apply a little heat so that they will start moving. Allow the ants enough time to relocate themselves. It may take some time for the last ant to leave the test tube. But once they are completely relocated, close your formicarium opening access and start to provide your ants with good nourishment and needed care.

With an AC standard test tube that has a hybrid nest, it is quite easy to transfer your ants. Simply connect the test tubes and the ant farm together and allow the ants some time to move in. Be warned that the moving in process may not happen immediately. Some ants may move completely within a day while some may take weeks or months to move. Ordinarily, ants do not leave their nest without any good reason. So, you may experience a situation where they do not want to move because they are comfortable where they are. When this happens, you should not worry. You only have to make them move by yourself.

Apply light heat on the test tube or touch the test tube with a cold towel. When they feel uncomfortable or disturbed, they will want to leave the old home.

Note that you may keep one or more queens in a formicarium. It all depends on their species. Some ants are monogynous and thus can only have one queen in a colony. There are also polygynous species. In this family of ants, more than one queen can establish a colony. Certain polygynous species go through what is known as pleometrosis in which the queens that raise the first set of workers fight each other until only one survives. In some families of these ants, the workers will murder all the queens except one. The fight among queens can have a terrible and devastating consequence for the surviving queen. Some are so wounded that they die afterwards, leaving the entire colony without a queen. So, before you keep two queens together in a nest, it is of crucial importance that you take time to study the species. If they are a monogynous species, don't put them together in a nest.

Similarly, you cannot keep two colonies of ants of the same or different species in the same ant farm with or without their queens. This is because they will fight each other. Ants are always conscious of their colony. Thus, two ants from different colonies are likely to fight even if they are of the same species. Besides, ants from different families do not behave in the same manner and feed on different things. Some ants keep slaves, some are thieves, some are farmers and herders, you name it... So, it is not advisable to keep and raise ants of different species in one formicarium to avoid one killing the other.

Children and Ant Colony Management

Some parents wouldn't buy ants for their children to keep as pets because of the fear that they can be stung or exposed to infection. The truth is that some children are ant enthusiasts and they can care for a colony of ants. But some have no interest in ants. So, it all depends on whether or not your child has interest in ants and on his/her sense of responsibility as well as age. So, if your child has interest in ant keeping and he or she can handle the task, there is nothing wrong in allowing him or her to have an ant colony. But remember that children are not adults. So, don't expect him/her to behave like an adult. You should therefore monitor them. Besides, it is important that you consider the species in question. I would advise against a child handling invasive and stinging ants. He/she can make a mistake that may lead to the escape of the ants from their colony and can be stung.

Chapter 6. Taking Care of Your Ant Colony

Like every other living thing, ants also eat. If you are keeping them in captivity, you have to provide them with proper nutrition otherwise they will all die. What do ants eat? How do they find their food? Do your ants require water to live? What diseases and parasites affect them? In this chapter, I am going to provide answers to these and other questions about ant care.

Ant's nutrition

In the wild

Ants are omnivorous by nature. While in the wild, they move around in search of insects and their eggs. They also steal the milk of small Hemiptera including aphids, eat wild fruits and lick the sap of plants. When they scavenge in the bins around the home, they feed on animal food and fats, sweets, dairy products, meat and others. Ant colonies have groups of workers that search for food for the rest of the colony. I am going to explain to you how they search for food in one of the subtitles of this chapter. As already mentioned above, some ant species practice vampirism. There are some queens that eat their workers, especially if they are stressed or as a result of some environmental factors. Most queens at the founding stage of a new colony feed their larvae with their eggs.

Ants feed on liquid foods. Foragers take solid foods to their colonies for the nourishment of their larvae (I will explain this later). However, they do not take liquid foods home as they do not have containers to put them in and transport. However, they still do not eat such foods alone. You may be wondering how they are still able to share such types of food. Mother Nature has provided ant foragers with two stomachs, their individual stomachs and community stomachs. The latter is larger than the former. When they find liquid foods outside, they consume them. The liquids are stored in the community stomach. When they get back to their nest, they

76

regurgitate these liquids and share with others. Their body mechanism will move some of these liquids to their individual stomachs (crops) for their own nourishment. The rest will be given out for the nourishment of other members of their colony. Foragers provide more foods to the larvae that will become queens while those that will become workers are given a smaller quantity. They also provide food to their queen as she does no work except lay eggs.

How do ants sense food?

If you are observant, you would have noticed that no matter where you keep food for your ants in the outworld, they will definitely find it. The same thing happens in the wild or when ants enter your home. No matter where you hide your food insofar as the environment is favorable for their survival and the food appeals to them, they eventually find it. How does this happen? The first thing that I would like you to know is that every food, including sweets and sugar has a unique odor. Ants are able to perceive these odors even from afar. However, the distant at which the smell of food dissipates differs from food to food. Some can be perceived by ants from a distance of 3 or 5 meters (9 to 15 feet). For example, desert ants are able to perceive the aroma of dry biscuit crumbs from a distance of three meters (9 feet). Thus, once they perceive the smell, they begin to move towards it in search of the food. Ants also have a strong sense of touch. When they touch a food source, they can determine whether or not it is edible.

Foragers do not look for food as a group but individually. Some foragers can travel up to a distance of 100 to 200 meters (300 to 600 feet) in search of food. In the wild, what determines how long they will travel is the time of the year. They also consider their territorial limits when searching for food. Each forager moves randomly. But as they move, they leave the chemicals pheromones on their trails to enable them locate their way back with the smell of these chemicals. Once it is approaching a food source, it will perceive the odor with the help of its antennae. There are hair-like sensilia in the antennae of each ants. These organs have sensory neurons. These sensory neurons have other parts such as glomeruli that make it possible for them to perceive odors.

The forager will locate the food source but it will not start feeding immediately. It will only collect a little sample and hurry to the colony, taking the shortest trail. It will drop the food for other ants to analyze it. If it is good for the colony, they will send other foragers to help in bringing the food inside the colony. As already explained above, the number of scouts to be sent depends on the quantity of food. If the food is plenty, many foragers will be sent to bring it in. But if it is not plenty, only a few of them will be sent.

I mentioned in a chapter above that ants go to school. The food finding process is one of the things that foragers learn. Ants do not find foods through an intuitive process. Have you ever seen two or three ants moving about circuitously with one of them leading the way and the other following her behind? The ant in front is an experienced forager and those behind are learning the act of foraging from her. This paired march is referred to as tandem running in ant keeping. You will notice that occasionally the group will stop momentarily and continue their movement afterwards. The reason for the stop is to enable the inexperienced scout to note and mark the landmarks. When the inexperienced ant has committed the landmarks to her memory, she will tap the abdomen and hind legs of her master twice and they will continue in their tandem running. In this learning process, the master ensures that her student is catching up. So, if she runs faster than her students, she will wait for them to come closer before she will continue. Any time you see a pair of ants working in this manner, I would want you to perform one experiment. Just get a hair. Once the two stop, tap the ant in front on her abdomen or hind legs with the hair. You will see that the leading ant will start to move. You have deceived her with the touch. She thinks that her student is ready to continue the march.

Now that you have learnt the feeding process of ants while in the wild, I am going to tell how you should feed the ants in your ant farm.

Feeding ants in captivity

When you take ants into captivity, they also replicate these feeding processes. The major difference is that the foragers take home what they can find in the outworld (unless their outworld is the outside world). In other words, their movement is limited to the food sources they can get. They depend so much on what you provide for them. So, it is necessary to provide them enough food and also in variety. Though ants eat everything, it is also advisable that you provide them with nutritious foods. They need two major food substances, namely, protein and sugar. Protein is very important for a colony that has a queen. This is because the queen requires protein in order to lay more eggs. The larvae also need protein in order to grow. Sugar is a good source of energy.

Since your workers require energy for work, they will also need sugar for that. To make their foods more balanced and nutritious, I will suggest that you mix the foods so that they will have variety and also obtain a variety of food nutrients. Protein sources that you can add to their meals include meat, honeydew surrogate, free amino acids, protein whey and others while the sugar sources are honey, maple syrup, honey water, sugar water and fruits such as oranges, grapes, apples and others. You can also provide them with insects such as fruit flies.

Note that certain foods are not good for your ants. Don't provide them with foods that easily rot or sticky food to avoid the risk of ants getting stuck. For example, honey is highly nutritious. But it is not advisable that you provide them with such a food. This is because it is sticky. Let me emphasize this, don't provide your ants with insects obtained from sites that may be treated with insecticides or pesticides. This is because it is more likely that the insects have already contacted the chemicals. If this is the case, the chemicals will also affect your ants. They may end up dying. If you are not sure whether or not insecticides have been sprayed in a location, don't catch insects from the area. Rather, you should purchase mealworms and crickets from a pet store.

Ants can become infected with mites, parasites and certain diseases through the foods they consume. Thus, I will recommend that you keep your ants' food in a refrigerator for a couple of hours before meal time. However, you don't have to leave it in freezers for many hours. Though nothing will happen to the food when they are left in the freezer for many hours, the food can spoil if it is melted repeatedly. To avoid thawing foods repeatedly, I will suggest that you divide the foods into various portions with each portion being enough for the ants per meal. Thus, you melt and serve them with a portion once you bring it out from the fridge. There shouldn't be any left over.

If you have live insects, you can kill them with hot water to give them a painless death before serving your ants. Just boil water with a microwave or stovetop and then drop them inside the water. By boiling the insects, you may kill any parasites like mites on them. It can also weaken any insecticides or pesticides within them – if there are any. This depends on the type of chemical used as insecticides or pesticides. Thus, boiling the insects does not give 100% positive result.

How to feed your ants
Ants are not like other types of pets. You cannot just drop or keep food for them as you may end up causing their death. They can drown by certain foods. Food can get messy and provide a favorable environment for mold to survive if they are not properly served. This is why it is of crucial importance that you learn how to feed your ants. The first point I have to mention here is that adult ants don't eat solid foods. Therefore, you have to offer them more liquid foods or foods in the form of porridge or a soft paste. If you are providing them with mealworms, cut them open so that the ant can go to the

main meal immediately. Dab a cotton plug on the liquid food and then put it in a test tube and keep in your ants' in the foraging area. You may also consider putting the food in small dishes and then keep the dishes at the basin of your ant farm. With these methods, the basin does not get messy and cleaning will also be easier for you.

Another important factor to take into consideration in the feeding of your ants is that like human beings, ants do not like eating the same type of food every day. They like variety. Providing them with various kinds of foods will help to improve the nutritional value of their food. This is because each food offers different nutrients and taste to the ants.

What to feed your ants
Pet stores have different kinds of food for ants. You can also obtain some food from your home. But bear in mind that each species of ants has their own preference when it comes to feeding. Some ants like sweets and sugars. For this species, apples, oranges, bananas, a mixture of honey and water and the likes are good options. There are yet other species that like consuming fruits and vegetables (they are vegetarian). These species of ants, such as harvester ants, feed on fruits and seeds. Some Ants are carnivorous in nature. They eat more of insect larvae and caterpillars. If you are keeping an ant colony of this kind of ant family, you should consider providing them with crickets and other kinds of insects.

Thus, it is advisable that you first find out the type of food that your ant will like and then provide then with such food. But regardless of the species of ants that you are keeping and raising from home, you should not forget to provide them with water, otherwise they will die. However, you should be very careful in doing that. Some beginners have ended up drowning their ants. Though, it is important that you provide your ants with drinking water, you don't have to use a bowl or similar types of containers. Ants are very tiny and they can drown in a spoonful of water. A very good way of providing them with water is to put some water in a test tube and then insert some cotton inside it to stop it from pouring out and also to prevent the ant from falling inside the water. They can drink from the cotton.

There are a number of things that you can add to your ants' food in order to boost its nutrient content. Personally, I provide my ants with multivitamins to increase their vitamin and mineral intake. Adding crushed chewable vitamins to their foods will make it very nutritious. Depending on the species of ant you have, you may add a little vinegar to your ants' food in order to prevent mold from developing on it as the ants consume them. If you provide your ant with food mixed with vinegar, you should observe your ant's reaction. Some species of ants do not like vinegar at all and so if you mix their food with it, they will not eat it.

Adult ants and solid food
It is highly probably that you have seen ants gathered around solid foods or foragers taking solid foods inside their colony. Thus, it is not abnormal if you are surprised to read that adult ants do not feed on solid food. No conclusive research has been conducted on this. Some experts still believe that ants, or at least some species of ants, can eat solid foods. But popular opinion on this is that adult ants do not eat solid foods because of their morphology. Ants have a thread waist, that is the gap between their altirunk and gaster is constricted, making it impossible for solid food to pass through to get to their digestive system. Thus, they feed on liquids such as sugary secretions of plants and bugs and hemolymph of insects. But the question to be asked is why are adult ants carrying solid foods inside their homes? What are these solid foods for?

Surprisingly, the larvae of ants consume solid foods as they fit through their digestive system. Since they require a lot of food, especially protein substances, to grow, foragers bring them solid foods from outside. Thus, foragers fill their community stomach and still come back with solid food for the nourishment of the larvae. So, when you see an adult ant carrying solid foods, it is meant for their larvae. Some species of ants do store strained out solid foods in their buccal cavity to be used when needed. For example, leaf-cutting ant queens start the first fungal garden of their colony with fungal pellets stored in their buccal cavity. However, not every solid food carried by these little creatures is meant to serve as food. A special group of workers also go out to bring building materials for the construction of more chambers or nestling areas in their colony.

Feeding a queen

Feeding a queen that is about to establish a colony is quite different from feeding a colony. The type of nourishment to be provided depends on the type of queen being raised. Each of the three types of queens has her unique nutrition requirements. If you are keeping a fully-claustral queen, you don't have to bother yourself about her nourishment. They can live for many months without taking external food. This does not mean that they do not eat. They obtain nourishment from the fats and other food substances stored in their body. Their body system can also metabolize their wing muscles to get nourishment from there. However, you can provide them with nourishment if you want. But note that they will prefer to feed on sweets such as maple syrup, honey, sugar-water and the likes to feeding on insects, though some species of fully-claustral queens like Aphaenogaster queens can also feed on insects during this foundation stage in the life of her colony.

Semi-claustral queens will require food at this initial stage. This is why their test tube is normally left open and put in a box where food is kept for the queen. She will search for food when she is hungry and will eventually find it and take it to her test tube. You can provide her with sugar. But if her eggs have hatched into larvae, I will recommend that you provide her with more protein for quick growth of her first brood.

Note that the nutritious needs of nanitics ants are slightly different from those of queens. You can feed them on sugar and other kinds food.

Health Concerns of Ants

Just like other living creatures, ants can have some health problems and other challenges that can constitute a threat to their existence. If these concerns are not properly handled, the queen and her workers may be affected adversely. I am going to discuss a couple of these challenges.

Fungi infection

Ants can be infected by fungi of different kinds such as molds, insect-infecting Aspergillus flavus, zombie-ant fungus and others. Some of these fungi can affect the general wellbeing of your ants and their queen. They can even cause their death. The best way to avoid fungi infestation is to keep your formicarium clean. Though ants are capable of maintaining high self-hygiene, the nature of their home in captivity can give rise to fungi infection. Fungi like mold are everywhere. They will start developing once the environment favors their survival. Thus, you have to make your ants' living environment unfavorable for their survival. If mold eventually develops in your ant farm, the best thing to do is to relocate the colony to another formicarium and then clean up the mold and apply disinfectants in and around the ant farm before you can begin to use it again.

As I already mentioned, fungi infections can result in the death of ants. If you discover that your ants are dying, you can carry out a simple experiment to find out whether the death is caused by fungi. Collect the dead ants and keep them covered in a container. Leave them in the lidded container for several days to see if fungi will develop on them. If you can spot a visible sign of any fungi, then it is likely that there is fungus infection in your ant colony. But if the contrary is the case, chances that the deaths are as a result of a fungus infection are very slim. Some species of harmful fungi live inside the body of their victims. Thus, you will not see any visible sign of fungus infection in your colony but they are gradually decimating your ants.

Bear in mind that not all fungi are harmful to ants. For example, some species of fungus, such as red fungus, normally sprout on ant farms made from plaster of Paris after a period of time. But no harmful effect has been associated with them when they develop in a colony of ants in a formicarium. I have spotted this red fungus in a nest of my ant colony made from POP. But nothing happened to my ants. Many ant keepers have had similar experiences.

Parasites

Parasites like mites can infect an ant colony. There are several ways through which such parasites can find their way into an ant colony. First, they can enter your formicarium through the food you provide your ants with. Feeding your ants with contaminated food can result in a parasite infestation. Some queens may have these parasites on them when they are captured. Thus, as they populate their colonies, parasites also continue to spread to other members of the colony. Inspect your queen and other ants very well to see if they have mites on them. Mites are very much tinier than ants. Thus, they can live on their bodies. Look closely at your queen to see if you can spot a dot-like creature. Also check the walls of your ant formicarium for such tiny creatures. If you can spot any, it is very much likely that your ants have a parasite infestation.

If there are parasites in your ant farms, I regret to tell you that there may not be any remedy for now. There are insecticides and pesticides that can eliminate mites. But the problem is that most of them – if not all of them – can also kill ants. However, some mites do no harm to insects. Besides, ants are also intelligent creatures. They can devise means of handling these parasites.

Apart from mites, there are also some parasitic wasps and flies that can kill ants. Some of these flies lay their eggs inside the body of ants or on their bodies. When these eggs hatch, they become destructive, eating up the gaster of the host. When the gaster is destroyed, the ant will die and the parasites will complete the damage by eating the remains of their victim. Again, it is so sad that not much can be done to eliminate these flies or prevent them from attacking ants for now. Worse still, there is no way to determine whether they are present in an ant colony or not. If you find such parasitic flies in your ant colony, you can take them to the lab for experts to study and identify them. They can provide you with useful tips on how to take care of them or prevent them from attacking your ant colony again.

Constant brood death

Some ant keepers have reported that their brood kept dying even when everything was alright with the queen and the mature workers. Some have also observed that even though their queens were laying eggs constantly, their broods were not increasing in number. They kept disappearing. These things do happen often. But there are a number of factors that can cause them. First, the brood can die as a result of environmental factors such as too much cold, dryness and unfavorable living environment. Just as some moms are not good mothers, there are also some queens that are not good moms. They can devour some of their broods as a result of stress and also environmental issues. So, if your brood keep disappearing or diminishing in population, then you need to observe the queen very closely. Take note of their living environments to see if there are some factors that make it not conducive for the queen. If everything is fine and there is no atom of disturbances such as vibrations, it is likely that your queen is not a good mother. You can leave her in isolation until her death.

Note that some queens normally lay eggs and feed the larvae with them. There are also some species of queens that lay eggs just to eat them. A typical example of such species of queen is a Formica queen. I don't consider such queens as bad mothers because it is simply their nature.

Breeding Your Ants' Food

You can save money on your ant food by breeding your own live insects rather than purchasing them from a pet shop. There are different kinds of live ant foods that you can breed from your home. Here, I will only limit our discussion to the rearing of crickets to use as ants' food from your home.

Breeding crickets

You will require a container to breed crickets from home. This will serve as the home for the crickets. I will recommend that you get two containers. You will keep baby crickets in one container and then adults in the second container. A transparent lidded container will be ok. The size of the container depends on the number of crickets that you would like to keep inside it. For example, More than 500 crickets can be kept in a container of 53 liters. Enough egg crates or cardboard should be added to the container for the crickets to climb on. The tote surface should be smooth in order to prevent the crickets from escaping or to reduce the number that will escape. The tote box has to be airy so that the crickets will not suffocate to death. So, you can create one or two holes of about six inches each on the lid of the tote as channels through which air comes into the container. Use a metal mosquito screen to cover the holes so that the crickets will not escape from captivity.

You can secure the screen using a hot glue gun. If you want more control over the heat, try variable vents. Insulate the bottom of the tote bin with 1 to 2 inches (2.54 to 5.08cm) of dry vermiculite. This material also minimizes odor, forestalls the growth of bacteria and also provides a suitable platform for the crickets to walk. The vermiculite should be changed after half a year or even after a month, depending on how dense your colony is. Fill a disposable plastic container with very moist, damp, loose top soil and place it in the tote bin. The container should not be higher than the vermiculite to make it possible for the crickets to jump in and out of it. The plastic container will serve as a breeding place for female. Ensure that the top soil to be poured on the container does not have pesticide, insecticide or fertilizer on it. Cover the soil with a screen so that crickets will not consume the eggs or burrow on the soil. The females will make use of their ovipositor (egg laying spike) to place their eggs via the screen.

You can start off with 50 or more crickets. Purchase both males and females. But the females should be of a greater number than the males so that your colony will grow. Place the crickets in the container and feed them with potato slices, fruit, greens and other kinds of vegetables. Provide your crickets with water using an inverted bottle reptile water dispenser, unflavored jello or a dish water gel. Put a sponge in the reservoir so that the crickets will not drown themselves as they attempt to drink the water.

To enhance breeding and facilitate the incubation of eggs, it is advisable that you keep your colony warm. There are different means of heating the container. You can use a light bulb, heat pad or a reptile heater. For optimal performance and wellbeing of crickets, the tote bin housing the cricket should have a temperature of about 80 to 90 degrees Fahrenheit. Once the environment and conditions are favorable for survival, it will take about 20 weeks for adult female crickets to lay eggs. Remove the disposable plastic container once you notice that they have laid their eggs and then replace it with another one so that they will continue laying eggs and providing you with more brood.

Crickets normally provide warmth to incubate them to hatch. So, you have to incubate the eggs by yourself by providing them with heat. Just put the disposable container containing the eggs in another bigger container with a lid. Seal the container very well and keep it in a secure place. But ensure that the temperature of any place where the container is kept is between 85 and 90 degree F. If this temperature is maintained throughout the incubation period, the eggs will start hatching after two weeks. Make a home for them as described above and keep them there. When they are grown to maturity, you can use them as food for your ant colony.

Other living ant foods that you can raise from home include roaches, termites, springtails, aphids, crickets, red flour beetles, mealworms and others. Breeding your ants' foods by yourself increases your workload. So, you can only go into that if you have the strength or if you will be able to meet the challenges. But on the positive side, you will have the opportunity of observing other insects and learning how they behave. It can be fun keeping these tiny creatures. Another advantage of breeding your ant colony's food by yourself is that it gives you the peace of mind that your ants are fed with uncontaminated foods or foods that are free from any parasitic infestation, since you breed them by yourself.

Recipe for a Delicious Food for Ants

I am going to teach you a formula for preparing delicious and nutritious paste for ants. I have fed many species of ants with this food and they all enjoyed it. Definitely, your ants will also like it if you give them this paste.

Things you will require:

- Canned chicken (preferably organic)

- Organic honey

- Hummingbird nectar

- Water

- High speed blender

The recipe
Open the canned chicken and remove the liquid content. Pour purified water inside the can and put it in a refrigerator for a while. Bring it out and remove the liquid content. Go through this stage over a couple of times or for about an hour. The chicken should have a mild taste when it is ready to be used. Put half cup of chicken in the blender and then pour one cup of purified water into the blender.

Put two tablespoonful's of hummingbird nectar and a tablespoonful of honey into the blender and then blend them together using the highest speed. Keep blending until a soft mixture is obtained. At this point, it is good to be served to the ants. Depending on the size of your colony, this quantity can serve them for two weeks. After each meal, refrigerate the liquid before serving again.

You can turn this liquid into an edible paste for your ants. You will require a microwave and modified food starch for this. Warm the liquid already obtained from the above process for thirty minutes. Add the modified food starch and stir to blend it very well with the liquid. The paste should not be very sticky otherwise you will not be able to draw it with a syringe. Once the mixture is well blended, refrigerate it and it is ready to be served. After each meal keep what is remaining in the refrigerator.

You can also turn the paste into cubes for ants. You will require some agar agar, which is available for sale in most supermarkets. Warm the paste for 30 seconds in a microwave. Though, you should not overheat it but it should be very hot. The paste will explode if you overheat it. When it is very hot, put two teaspoonfuls of the agar agar on the paste and turn it very well to obtain a perfect blend. If you like, put a teaspoonful of ReptaBoost to make it more nutritious. Pour the mixture in a flat container. The heap should be thin. Put it in a fridge to cool. When it is cool, cut it into cubes. Then put them in an air tight container and place it back in the refrigerator for longer storage.

There are other recipes for ant foods which I will not describe here because of lack of space. But you can look them up on the Internet. Making your ant food from scratch also has the advantage that you know it is not contaminated!

Cleaning Up Your Ants' Home

I have already mentioned above that ants maintain high body hygiene. They don't like living in a dirty environment. If you are keeping an ant colony, you have to clean their environment, especially the dumping site and foraging area. Cleaning your ant farm can be quite challenging, especially to a beginner. First, use cotton to seal the entrance of the nest before you start cleaning the outworld. Don't use a vacuum; otherwise you will frighten the ants in their nest. Scrub the dirt with a paint brush or wire. Try not to shift the ant farm to avoid disturbing the ants. If your outworld is wide enough, you can clean it up with a cloth. A barbecue skewer will be suitable for cleaning a narrow outworld.

What To Do To Facilitate the Growth Of An Ant Colony

There are three things that you must do to ensure the growth of your ant colony. First, you have to provide them with enough food. The food should be nutritious. Secondly, the heat condition of their nest should be favorable to their survival. You should know that ants are cold-blooded animals. Like other cold-blooded insects, warmth of their surroundings determines the rate at which they perform physiologically. I will recommend that you provide heat to the level of 25 to 27 degrees C to one side of the nest using a heating pad. This will make it possible for the ants to regulate themselves. They will move to the part of the formicarium that has the best warmth for their survival. Note that the majority of ants from locations of tropical climates will survive only for a few months at constant room temperature. They need a location where they can warm up. However, you should be very careful in the process so that you do not end up burning your ant. Don't expose the ants to the sun. Proper heat and nutrition engender more egg production. Third, you have to ensure that your ant's living environment is clean and tiny. Don't allow mold to develop in their home otherwise you will be exposing them to a fungi infestation.

Chapter 7. General Information about Ant Keeping

There is a lot to be learnt about ant keeping, especially if you are a beginner. In this chapter of this book, I am going to provide you with general ant keep tips and a glossary of terminologies used in ant keeping.

General Tips and Tricks

I am going to provide some general ant keeping tips to help you get started anytime you want to establish your own ant colony.

Before establishing any ant colony, I will advise you to first of all learn about ants, various species and their behavior. With a good knowledge of ants, you will definitely be a better ant keeper.

- Know what the laws on ant keeping are as well as other exotic pets in your locality before you order ants.

- Make sure that you have a suitable house. A good ant farm should replicate, to a considerable extent, the natural environment of the species of ant that you want to keep.

- Ensure that there is enhanced air circulation in your formicarium. You can do that with an air pump. This will help to prevent the test tube from becoming moldy.

- Whether you want to relocate a colony to a new home or you are transferring them from test to an ant farm, you can easily accomplish that and make them cooperate by putting them for a minute in a refrigerator. This will help to make them less active. Normally, when any container or ant formicarium containing ants is touched, the ants inside it will begin to move about and scatter as they search for escape as a result of fear. But if you chill them, they will be weak to move about and this will make it easy for you to move them.

- When you want to move a small colony to another test tube because their initial home is dirty or has become moldy, you can take advantage of light or sunlight. Bring a new test tube where you will be moving them and wrap it in foil. Then, get it connected it to the moldy one where they have been staying, by wrapping foil around the two open ends. Then bring out the closed end of the test tube you are moving them out from under the sun or apply light on it. But don't burn them. Just make their home somewhat uncomfortable. They will vacate the house to a more comfortable one. If you are using a nesting medium, it will also be possible for you to get them to dig up against a container using this method.

- Test tube caps are good examples of connectors you can use to join two tubes. Drill a hole into a test tube cap using a drill bit that is of similar size to the tubing you use. Plug cotton inside the hole when they are not being used. Through the hole, you will be able to connect and disconnect tubing as you wish. I have tried this before during moving and it worked. This is why I am recommending it for you. I have connected small tubes for small colonies or for the queen using this method. If the workers of your colony require a basin, you can connect it to the tube using this method.

- It is possible to increase your ants' number with other ants from outside the colony, even though experts are not agreed on this. Get the larvae or pupae of ants of the same species with yours from the wild and keep them in your queen's test tube for her to nurture them to maturity. You should limit the number of larvae or pupae you are bringing in to 8 so that your queen will be able to take care of them, since she is still alone. But bear in mind that there is the possibility of your queen eating them up. The brood can also be infected with parasites or any disease. If your queen has some workers already, you can also get few ants of the same species from the wild and add to them. However, it may also be possible that the newly introduced brood may not be useful to the queen or they will be killed by the other workers.

- Don't use tape or any other gummy adhesive on your ants' formicarium because they can get stuck on the tape. Personally, I prefer to use clay for a number of purposes. It is a very good adhesive and does not cause any harm to your ants. You can use it during moving to connect tubes. It is a good material to be used as the base of your test tubes. I also use it as the feeding tray for my ants.

- Take time to study your ants. Ants are not like other pets that you can play with. The fun lies in observing and learning from them. Ant keeping will amount to an exercise in futility if the keeper does not take time to observe and study the ants. Also, don't be afraid to experiment with your ants. Some of the things I wrote here are learnt from experience arising from experiments I have done. In ant keeping forums people share their experiences, some of which are born out of experiments. If these people are afraid to experiment with their ants, they will not be able to provide solutions to the forum members with some challenges. So, don't be afraid to create experiments on diets, ant farms, different species etc.

- Handle your ants with care. Don't keep your ant farm in any location that is exposed to the sun, otherwise you risk baking your ants. A formicarium exposed to the sun will turn to an ovum, especially during the winter period. When the temperature of your formicarium becomes too high, your ants will die. Similarly, don't keep your ant farm closer to a heat source such as fireplace, stove or lamp. These sources can heat up your ants' colony. Ants can be frightened just like any other creature. So, don't tilt or shake their formicarium. Whilst moving them, ensure that you don't turn their home upside down to avoid destroying their nest.

- Keep the ant farm out of the reach of children. Don't allow them to go to where you keep your ants alone for any reason. You should always be with them when they want to view your ants. Finally, don't allow any person to tap on or hit your ant's home with anything to avoid frightening them.

94

- Join an ant forum to learn more practical tips on ant keeping. If you search for ant keeping forums online, you will get an impressive results.

Ant Keeping Equipment You May Need

Ant keeping requires various kinds of tools and equipment, with each serving different purposes. Below are some of the tools and equipment that you may find useful as an ant keeper.

- Formicarium/ant farm

- Test tube

- Interposer kit

- Liquid ant feeder

- Spoon

- Tweezers and forceps

- Ant slip barrier

- Test Tube Bung

- Tank connector

- Feeding dish

- Plastic vial

- Rubber tank connector

- Ants mug and notebook gift set

- Flexible plastic tubing

- Nest cover

- Pipette

- Atomizer fine mist spray bottle

- Trigger spray bottle

- Escape prevention kit

Ant Keeping Web-stores

As mentioned above, there are a lot of web-stores that sell ants of different species and ant keeping equipment. In case you are not able to find any physical store in your locality or prefer shopping online, here are some of the well-known web-stores that deal with ants and ant keeping tools.

Note: at the time of printing, all these websites fully functioning. As the internet changes rapidly, some sites might no longer be live when you read this book. That is, of course, out of our control.

https://antsuk.com

http://www.antstore.net

https://www.gamergate.com.au

https://antkit.uk

https://www.antstore.net

http://www.antscanada.com

https://tarheelants.com

https://www.antmate.com.au

Ant Keeping Forums

Ant keeping is gradually gaining ground in the world today. Ant enthusiasts have started coming together to help each other, provide tips and share ideas. If you are a beginner in ant keeping or you have interest in it, I will suggest that you register with one or two ant keeping forums. You will find a number of them online. Below are some of the popular ones with good Google ranking.

http://antkeepingforum.com

http://www.antscanada.com

http://antfarm.yuku.com/

http://www.formiculture.com

http://antark.net/links/ant-forums

https://www.antkeepers.com

http://forum.antscanada.com

http://support.proboards.com

In case you have any concerns or issues not covered in this book, you will find these forums useful. Just post your concerns there and you will get a useful response from experienced members.

10 Common Mistakes in Ant Keeping

There are a lot of ant enthusiasts out there that have tried, without any success, to raise ants from their home. The majority of these people failed because of simple things that they didn't get right. It would have been a huge success and a rewarding experience for them if they have done their homework and got it right. If you have an interest in ant keeping, take note of these simple mistakes and avoid them.

1. Keeping and buying exotic species: If you want to be successful in ant keeping and avoid any problems, I will advise you not to keep an exotic species – species that are alien to your locality or region. Experience has shown that in most cases, these foreign species do not make it. This is because it is difficult to duplicate their natural environment and the climatic conditions they are used to in an ant farm. Thus, they die if they cannot adapt to the environment.

Secondly, keeping an exotic species is not good for the environment. Besides, it can also be illegal depending on your jurisdiction.

2. Overcomplicated outworld – Another mistake that some people make is to have an overcomplicated outworld or basin attached to their formicarium. It is common to see an outworld with many decorations, trees, stones and things of that sort. They may give it a visual appeal but they create some problems. The ants can hide in the outworld. Complicated design also makes cleaning difficult. A good design should be accessible for easy cleaning.

3. Bad setup: many people have problems because of the setup. The issue may be poor ventilation, poor humidity or temperature. Your ants will not do well if your formicarium has poor design without proper ventilation, humidity and temperature.

4. Failure to hibernate: I have talked about hibernation in a chapter above. Experience has shown that many people fail because they don't allow their ants to hibernate. As mentioned above, hibernation is a natural process and if you don't allow the ants to hibernate, you're disrupting the cycle and this can have a damaging effect on ants. Beside, hibernation helps to prolong the life of the queen as it gives her a break from egg laying. So, if you don't help your ant to hibernate, you are shortening the life cycle of your queen and entire colony.

5. Moving a colony into a formicarium too early: Some people make the mistake of moving their first colony into an ant farm when they are too young to handle life in a big environment. Ideally, you should transfer your queen with 20 of her brood. With about 20 workers, the queen will not be exposed to unnecessary stress. Note that a small colony may not adapt to life in a bigger space.

6. Insufficient sugar and protein and water: Not providing a colony with a balanced diet is another common mistake among beginners in ant farming. Check the chapter on nutrition to know what your ants require. In a nutshell, your ants require sugar, protein and water.

They should be provided in proper proportions for your ants for proper growth.

7. Keeping ants in an air conditioned room: Ants are cold blooded and this means that they cannot produce their own heat. Thus, it is not good to keep them in an air conditioned room. If you have no other space to keep them except in an air conditioned room, then you should try providing them warmth with a heating cable.

8. Not giving your queen enough privacy: Almost every beginner in ant keeping is guilty of this to a considerable extent. This is because of feelings of excitement in having a queen and wanting to see her build her colony. But experience has shown that it is better to leave the queen in a quiet place undisturbed. Seeing her often will subject her to a lot of stress, which may even cause her to eat her eggs. She may also die.

9. Catching too many queens: If you are hunting for a queen, avoid the temptation of catching too many queens. You can make do with three or five queens. If you catch many of them, you may not be able to manage them, especially if all are successful in raising their colony. Thus, it is advisable to catch just a few.

10. Lack of research beforehand: I have said it a number of times in this book, don't start ant keeping without first doing enough research on the species that you will want to keep. It is not good to keep a queen or a colony of ants that you don't know anything about. So, people just read that ants are very easy to keep. They just catch a queen and keep her in captivity. This is not the best practice. You may discover when it is late that her species is not what you want.

Chapter 8. Why Humans Should Stop Killing Ants

Many people don't like seeing ants around their homes and offices. Their presence sparks feelings of annoyance in these people. Ants have become a source of frustration for a lot of people because of their continual presence in the kitchen and the manner in which they contaminate our foods. Their presence in our home becomes more worrisome if they sting or are infectious. Thus, killing them does not matter to a lot of people. However, it is good that we all have a rethink of our conception and treatment of these little creatures. They play a very important role in our ecosystem. Given their roles in the ecosystem, humans are not more significant than them. I am going to explain here why ants are important creatures in the ecosystem and why they should not be killed by humans again.

The Role and Importance of Ants in the Eco System

Humans benefit from nature through a wide range of activities called the ecosystem services. There are basically four categories of the ecosystem services which include cultural, regulating, supporting and provisioning services. Mother Nature in each of these categories does a lot of things for us human beings free of charge. The ecosystem services are very crucial for our survival on earth, even though there are a lot of other creatures that pay the price and make these services possible. Ants are among these creatures that make significant contributions in the ecosystem services and in maintaining the well-being of humans without receiving any appreciation. I'm sure you will want to know the various roles ants play in the sustenance of the eco-system.

Agricultural role of ants

In the supporting category of the ecosystem services, ants work with our farmers and help in bringing about abundant harvests in ways that go unnoticed. These tiny creatures can make it possible for farmers to grow their crops in areas where farming will ordinarily result in no yield. How do they help farmers? Ants, and some other insects like termites, burrow and establish colonies underground. This enhances infiltration of water and air in the soil. It also improves the level of nitrogen in the soil. Evans and his group wrote a research article in 2011 in which an increase in wheat crop production was associated to the actions of ants. There are other research articles that provided evidence on the agricultural role of ants. Apart from making the soil more fertile, I would also want you to know that ants offer protection to the crops and plants in the farms.

Many species of ants feed on insects. Some of these insects have a parasitic relationship with plants. With ants around in the farm, these insects will cause little harm to crops. In this way, ants again help to increase plant yield.

Food source to humans
I know that this may sound strange to some people. But in reality, there are some species of ants such as honey ants that are edible. Some communities in Australia, Africa, Central America, Southeast Asia, South and Central America and China eat these ants. They are good unconventional sources of protein. Some of these communities prepare nutritious delicacies with both the larvae and adult ants of the edible species. Though I personally have not eaten ants, there are many people who have eaten them. Neelkamal Rastogi in 2011 has mentioned edible ants and communities in the countries mentioned above that eat ants. This is the contributive service of ants in the general ecosystem services.

Disease prevention
Ants are probably the last creature some people will think about when disease prevention is mentioned or when the regulatory ecosystem service is mentioned. If you are in this category of people, I am telling you to have a rethink. Some species of ants have pharmacological benefits. They have well-developed and strong

immune systems. Thus, pharmaceutical companies are now formulating antibiotics with ingredients obtained from ants.

As noted by Rastogi, some of these companies are conducting research on the use of ants for the treatment of such health conditions as asthma and arthritis. Traditionally, certain communities in some continents use ants for therapeutic reasons. A traditional society in Africa sutures with the mandibles of certain species of ants while in some Indian communities, gout and joint pain can be treated with a particular species of ant.

Cultural importance of ants
Ants also play some roles in the cultural category of the ecosystem service in a number of ways. In a chapter above, I have explained various lessons humans can learn from ants. Thus, ants contribute to the education of humans. You can also view them as a pastime or leisure activity.

The above are some of the roles ants perform in the ecosystem humans. So, next time you see an ant, don't be in a rush to crush them.

How Can Humans Avoid Killing Ants?
Indeed, it can be annoying to see these tiny creatures invading your home and eating up your sugar, sucking up your juice with some getting drowned inside it. However, given their importance in the ecosystem, I will advise you not to kill them any longer. You are doing great harm to the ecosystem when you murder ants. Some species of ants are difficult to control but some are not. You don't have to kill them with insecticides or pesticides. I will provide you with tips to apply in order to avoid killing them or tips to send them out of your house or office in a natural manner.

Don't provide them with food
Ants are everywhere and they have well trained foragers. Once you keep food that appeal to them, they are definitely going to find them

no matter where the food is. Nobody who does not have a formicarium intentionally provides food for ants unless as a bait to kill them. But people unintentionally keep food for them and attract them inside their homes. You can avoid this by maintaining a clean environment. Make sure that there are no crumbs or spills in your kitchen or dining room, otherwise you are inviting them.

Seal your refuse sacks

I will also advise you to seal your sacks. Ants are good scavengers. Given how tiny they are, they can penetrate into any bin through little openings. Besides, odor from crumbs, spillage and rotten food substances oozes out easily from uncovered dustbins. Ants will perceive this odor and they will head to the location where it is coming from to search for food. But when they are tightly sealed, the smell will circulate inside the bin. So, if you don't want to invite them in your home, tightly seal your sacks so that they will not be able to enter.

Put your food and pet food in a lidded container

As I have already mentioned, ants' size help them to enter through containers if they are not tightly sealed. So, ensure that the containers where you keep your foods are tightly sealed. In this way, even if they are able to perceive the aroma of the food, they will not be able to enter the sealed container.

Use natural repellent

There are some substances that naturally repel ants but do not kill them. If you find ants in your living space or office, you can apply these natural repellents such as vinegar, ground coffee, powdered chilli, cinnamon or cinnamon powder on the floor of your home and kitchen cabinets.

Cover and seal cracks

Check the walls of your home to see if there is any cracks and crevices on them. If there is, you have to seal them because some species of ants nest in such places. Thus, if you seal them, there will be no place for them to make their nest around your home. They will look for alternatives. Furthermore, you can look for their entry point and outline it with chalk. Chalk does not kill them but ants do not walk across chalk lines. So, by outlining their entrance with chalk, they will look for another place to stay.

Careful move their nest to an open area
Some ants are very stubborn and any can withstand any attempt you make to stop them from entering your home. So, if you have applied all the above strategies above and they are still coming, you have to locate their nest and move them to a suitable open place. But make sure that you don't kill them. Also, wear gloves because some species of ants can sting. Note that in some jurisdictions, the destruction of their natural habitat is forbidden by law. So, seek alternative means or approved means of removing such creatures from human habitation.

Glossary

Abdomen: the ant's body comprises of three major parts, which consists of the gaster, petiole, metasoma and propodeum.

Acidopore: the gaster of formicinae ants has an orifice at its tip called acidopore through which they emit acid in times of danger to defend themselves.

Alate: it is a sexually mature winged ants.

Altitrunk: the second main part of the body of the ant comprises of the thorax and propodeum.

Antennae: a pair of segmented sensory appendages on an insect's head. It is called antenna in the singular form. These sensory appendages are very flexible.

Anterior: towards the head or the front

Apterous: ants without wings

Bicolored: ants with two colors

Bilobed: partitioned into two lobes

Brood: baby ants. The term can be used to refer to eggs, larvae and pupae

Carina: an elevated keel or ridge

Caste: individuals in a colony with unique and similar behaviors

Chitin: The exoskeleton of arthropods is formed by a strong, safeguarding and semi-transparent substance which is known as chitin.

Cuticle: the non-cellular outer covering of the wall of an insect's body

Dimorphic: available in two different forms such as minor and major workers

Distal: the part most distant away from the body

Dorsal: the upper back or surface

Elaiosome: a nutritious appendage on seeds which ants find appealing

Epinoturn: the altitrunk's upper surface

Facets: the visual units of the compound eyes of an ant, which look like lenses

Formic acid: acid sprayed by ants. It is secreted in a poisonous gland of an ant

Funiculus: it is a constituent of antenna beyond the pedicel of the second segment of the body of ant which comprises of 3-11 smaller parts

Gaster: normally referred to as the abdomen, it is the remaining part of the abdomen which is enlarged more than others

Honeydew: the sugary secretion of insects that eat sap such as aphids

Humerus: the shoulder

Labrum: the mouthparts' uppermost part

Maxillae: the jaws' second pair folded underneath the maxillae

Mesonotum: the upper part of the thorax's middle part

Monomorphism: Workers' single caste within a species

Myrmencology: the scientific study of ants

Nanitics – the first set of workers a queen produced to start off her colony with

Pectinate: a comb-like structure

Polydomy: A colony with more than a nest.

Polymorphism: more than one caste of workers such as major and minor workers in a colony

Replete: a worker that stores food for the colony's use with a distensible crop

Scape: the antenna's first part

Sclerite: a part of the body with grooves and ridges setting it off

Sting: the gaster's sharp pointed tip used by ants to deliver venom or to sting

Tarsus: series of parts of the leg attached to the tibia

Vector: an organism that infests another with a pathogen

Vertex: it is the upper part of the head located between the eyes

Waist: another name for petiole

Worker: an infertile female ant that performs a particular function for the caste.